Sailor Jerry's
Tattoo Stencils II

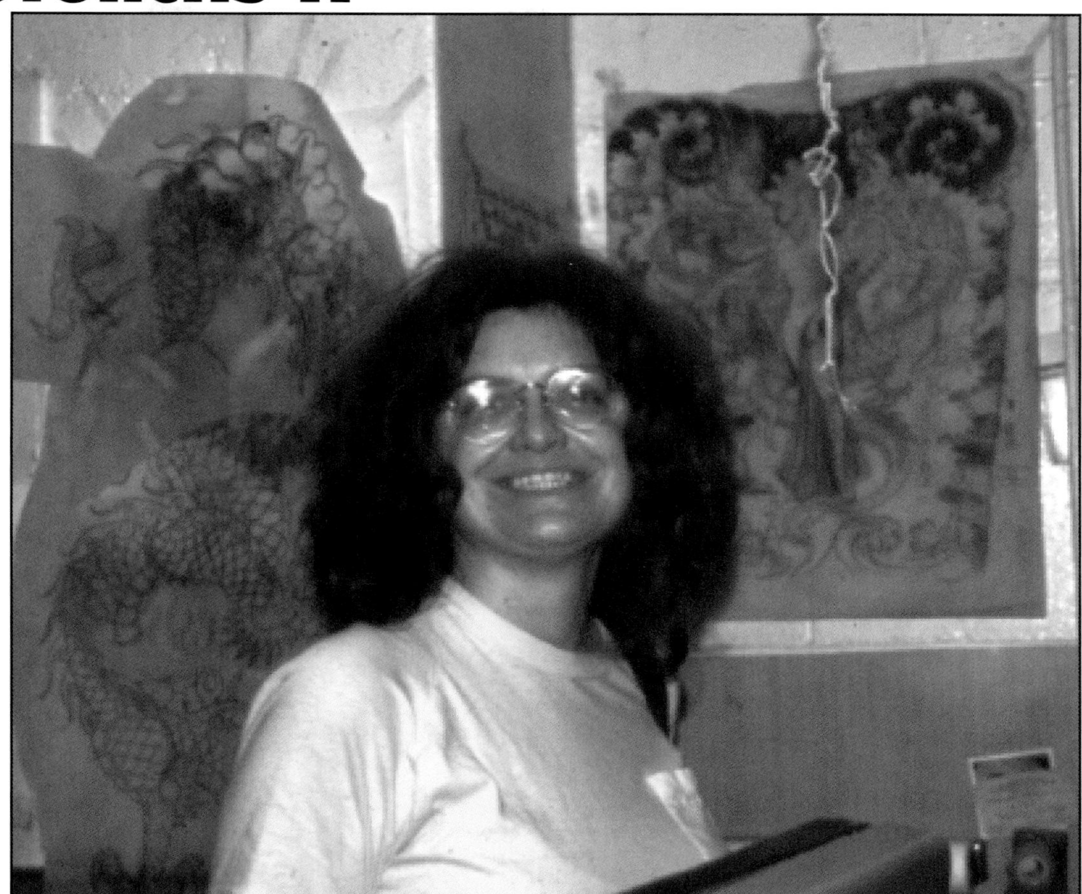

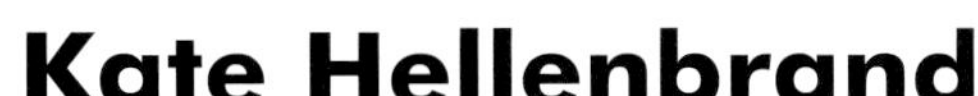
Kate Hellenbrand

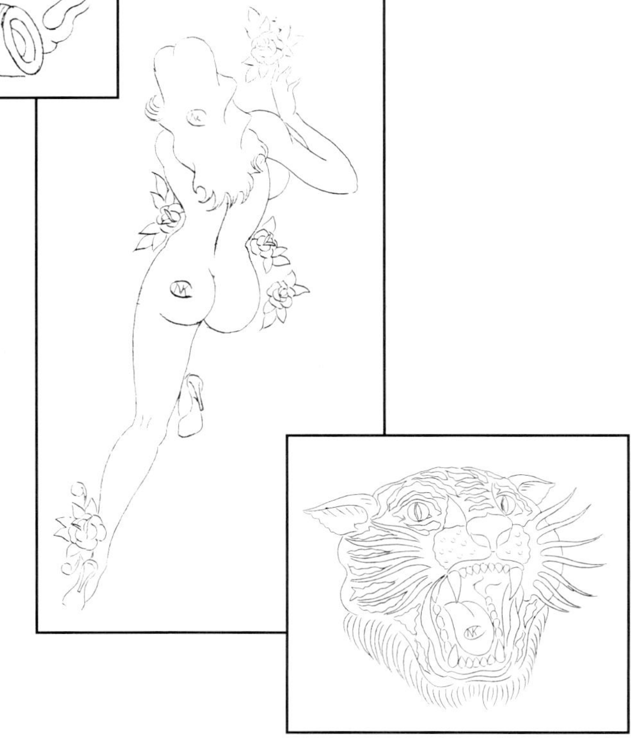

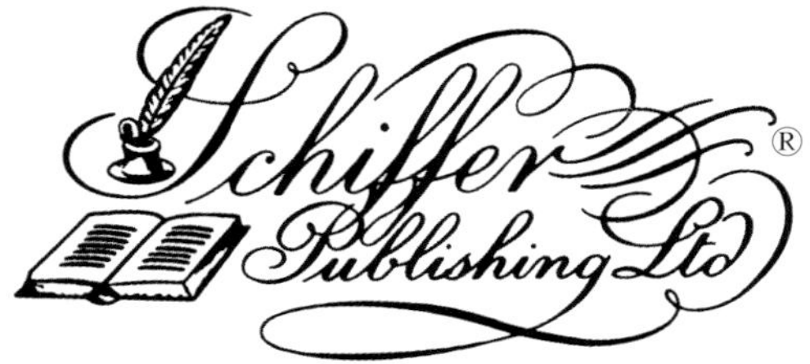

4880 Lower Valley Road   Atglen, Pennsylvania   19310

Dedication

For Megan Hall and Tim Hall — the keepers of the keys of my heart.
And for Zeke, wherever he may be.

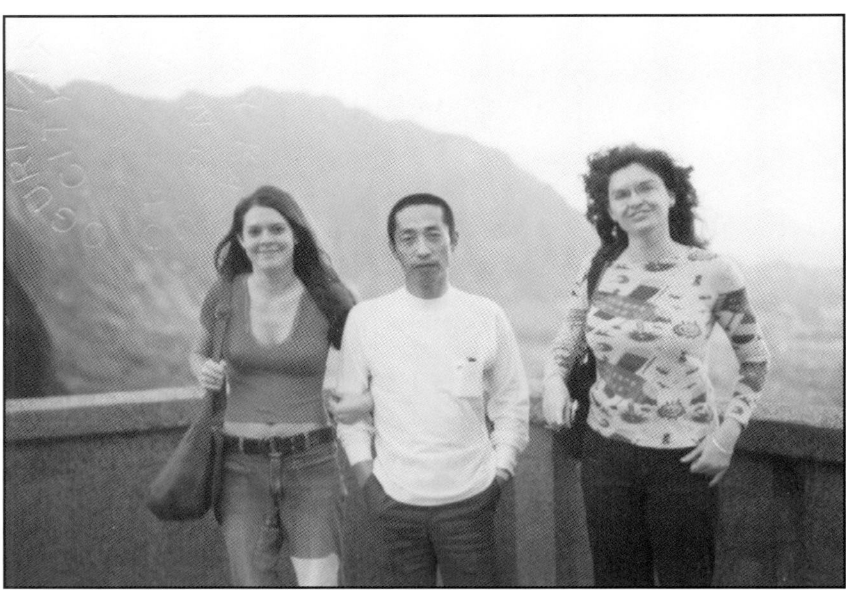

From left: The Council of the Seven participants: Mick (Sailor Jerry's apprentice); Kazuo Oguri; Kate Hellenbrand. Pali Overlook, Hawaii, 1972.
Photo courtesy of Sailor Jerry Swallow.

Front Cover: Sailor Jerry Collins. Photo from the collection of Kate Hellenbrand
Back Cover: Kate Hellenbrand. Photo: PF Bentley, PFPIX.com
Title page: Kate Hellenbrand in Sailor Jerry's shop, Honolulu, Hawaii, 1972

Library of Congress Card Number: 2002106903

Designed by Bonnie M. Henlsey
Cover design By Bruce M. Waters
Type set in Futura Md BT/CenturyOldst BT

ISBN: 978-0-7643-1655-5
Printed in China
7 6 5 4

Published by Schiffer Publishing Ltd.
4880 Lower Valley Road
Atglen, PA 19310
Phone: (610) 593-1777; Fax: (610) 593-2002
E-mail: Schifferbk@aol.com
Please visit our web site catalog at
www.schifferbooks.com
We are always looking for people to write books on new and related subjects.
If you have an idea for a book please contact us at the above address.

This book may be purchased from the publisher.
Please try your bookstore first.
You may write for a free catalog.

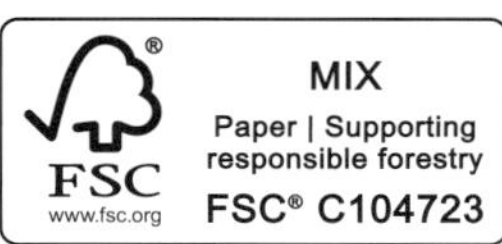

Contents

Acknowledgments

How does one convey adequate gratitude for a lifetime of help and support into a few brief paragraphs? Invariably, important people and contributions are overlooked. Let me say, then, thank you to everyone I've met along my way for their teachings. Each had a profound affect on my life's direction.

My special thanks go to Wes Wood for his support. I also extend my warmest thanks to the crew and staff at Sacred Tattoo in New York City — my fellow artists who display such passion for their craft and to the very busy floor personnel who watch out for us.

I applaud my clients who bring me their minds and bodies; I am nothing without their visions and trust.

I thank the people at Schiffer Publishing, especially Peter Schiffer who has opened his heart to my projects. Also Tina, Doug, Joe and all the smiling voices at the end of the phone. They continue to smooth over my anxious misgivings and bring my projects to light with the least amount of pain.

Personally, there are too many people to thank. To PF Bentley for his impeccable sense of timing and the great photographs, to Cathy Paypol for her help in letting the world know about my books, to Bill and Cynthia DeMichele for the photos and sales.

For my visionaries: Travis Johnson, Cory and Sarah Schaub; to Marc Alain Steier for the legal insights.

To my family who encouraged my curiousity and tolerated my adventures, especially my uncle, E. Dale Barton; my father, Waldo Barton; his wife, Margaret; and those who have traveled on before us.

A special shout-out to the Girl's Club: Jane Wallace; Merrily Ronniger; Debbie Ullman; Anna Sea; Julie Ward; Joan Sorensen; Jan Seeger; Pat Langmade; Kerri Rowe; Allison Goody; Sarah Spill; Cara Czekanski; Miss Anna Paige and all the convention cowgirls.

Big kisses to the Boys: Michael Corcoran; PF Bentley; Crag Rodriguez; Zsolt Sarkozi; Oliver Rutz; Danny and Oliver in Mexico City; the men on the road — old-schoolers and new kids on the block who inspire, especially Jack Rudy and Tony Olivas.

A tiny kiss to Cain Rhyolite.

A special note of gratitude to Tommy King of the Bronx who first gave me the gift of his living skin as canvas.

Thanks also to all of the artists who have put their energy and vision under my skin: Cliff Raven, Jack Rudy, Ed Hardy, Rob Koss, Bill Funk, Scott Sylvia, Mario Barth, Anil Gupta, Trevor Marshall, Aaron Caine, TJ Hernandez and Mike Wilson.

Most gratefully I thank Lyle Tuttle for this volume's introduction. As tattooing's tireless ambassador, he infuses our world with clarity and generous, gracious good humor. He is my hero.

And to all the people of New York City.

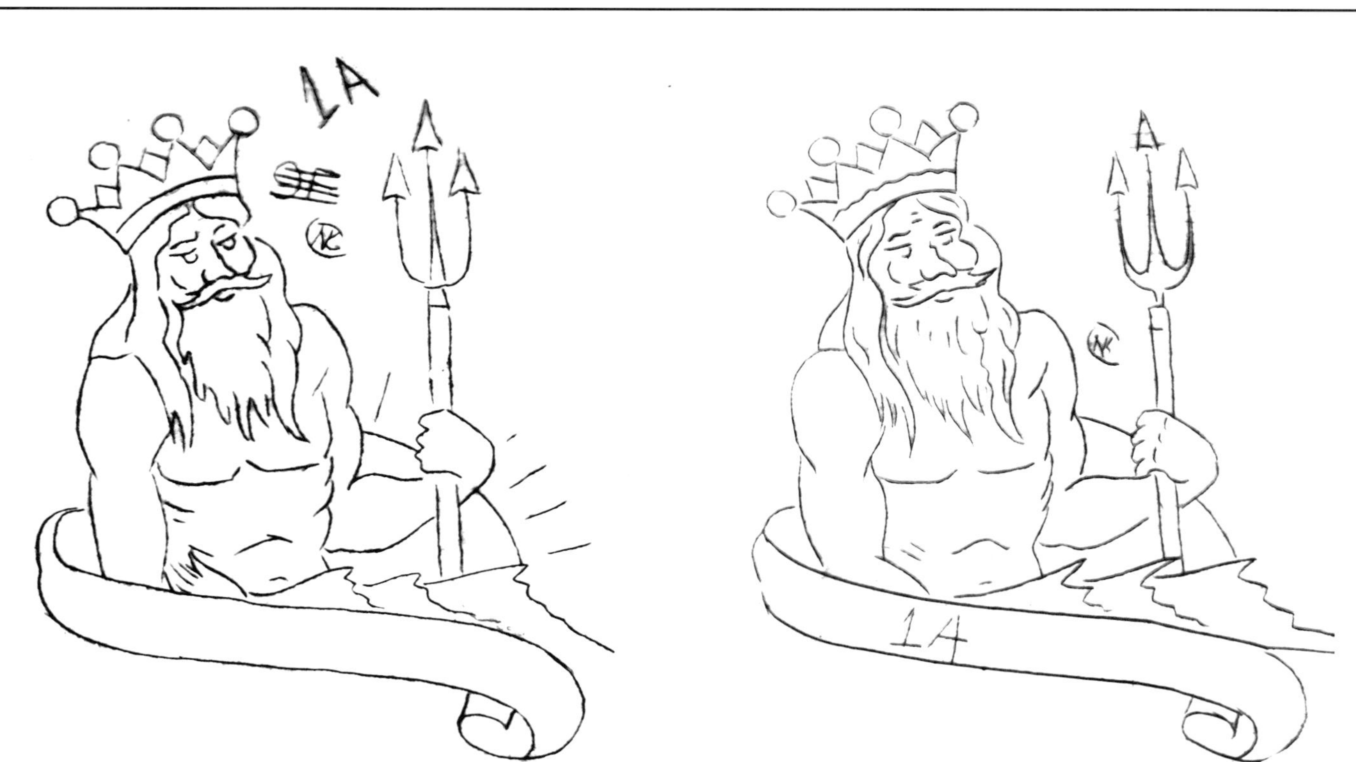

Can you find the ten differences between these two stencil images of the same design of King Neptune?

Both stencils were cut by Sailor Jerry, decades apart. To the left: the earlier Neptune shows more carbon in the grooves but a less accomplished drawing style. The 1A and scratched out 9F refer to Sailor Jerry's filing system. Below is the NKC, his signature. The filing number and signature appear on both stencils.

The differences: the sharpness of the pitchfork's shaft; the bulk of the pitchfork prongs; the sophisticated treatment of the hair, beard, eyes, wrinkles, hand, elbow, waves. Also note the smoothness of the lines on the banner. These are good examples as to how stencils continued to evolve favorably over constant recutting.

Preface

On September 11, 2001, I stood on my rooftop and watched with shock and horror as America came under attack from foreign forces for the first time since December 7, 1941.

When Pearl Harbor was attacked, I was not yet born. Yet I was greatly affected by the Second World War. My father was in the army and contracted tuberculosis while fighting. I didn't see him for the first 15 years of my life as he was highly contagious and confined under quarantine in a sanitorium after the loss of his left lung.

The conflict in Korea came with little consciousness from me but it supposedly was a "police action" and not a real war anyway.

Vietnam, however, was not only America's most unpopular war but also mine. It was the 1960s, I was young, and in the Summer of Love, too many young men were dying in a war that could not be defended.

On September 11th, I saw with my own eyes that evil does live, hiding in fundamentalism and caves. The audacity of the attacks on two of the biggest buildings in the world caused a paradigm shift in my long-term ambiguity about conflict. Routing out extremists who go to all lengths to twist the world to their narrow perspective must be a priority.

For the following three days I had only my internet account to keep in touch. I was unable to use my phone or subway system. On Friday, I was able to go back to the tattoo shop.

The first tattoo that I was asked to do was an American flag on one of the rescue workers who had been working in that pit of twisted iron and shattered concrete, looking for some sense or survivor.

Day after day after day went by. Getting to work was like living the same funeral over and over again, a loop of despair, confusion, debris, death. Thousands of people clogged the sidewalks yet there was no sound. Truck after truck came out of the restricted area, bumper to bumper, their huge flatbeds piled with the skeletons and skins of my beloved Twin Towers. (My shop's doors are only 20 feet way from the intersection of West Broadway and Canal, the official boundary line of access.) Media, mourners, memorials, heroic men and women and dogs — this was the daily obstacle course I ran going to and from my shop — for the next three months.

Then tourists began to come, the memorials faded away, New York City began to rebuild and become again the Mecca of art and culture. My business is getting back to normal. And through it all, people continue to ask for flags, for eagles, patriotic designs that will remind them of this time, this act, the freedoms they have as American citizens.

I began tattooing when military designs were the bread and butter of the business. Because Vietnam was my touchstone of what these images meant, I was often ambivalent in their application. I am surprised to learn how much I love doing them now.

I am surprised to learn how much I love my country, my fellow citizens, my adopted city. I have also rediscovered my intial pride in being a tattoo artist. It is an honor to embellish a body with these symbols of freedom.

I am proud to continue this story.

Kate Hellenbrand
New York City
December, 2001

P.S. The Navajo women, whenever weaving a rug, always leave one intentional mistake in the pattern. They say it "lets the evil out." My first volume of Sailor Jerry acetate tattoo stencil designs was due on September 15th, 2001. Obviously, on September 11th, my world collapsed into chaos. The rest of the world still had deadlines to keep, including my book's publication. I was, incidentally, reported as one of the missing from the World Trade Center's attack — number 3835. If there are any errors in the last volume of stencils, let them release any evil back on those who perpetrate it.

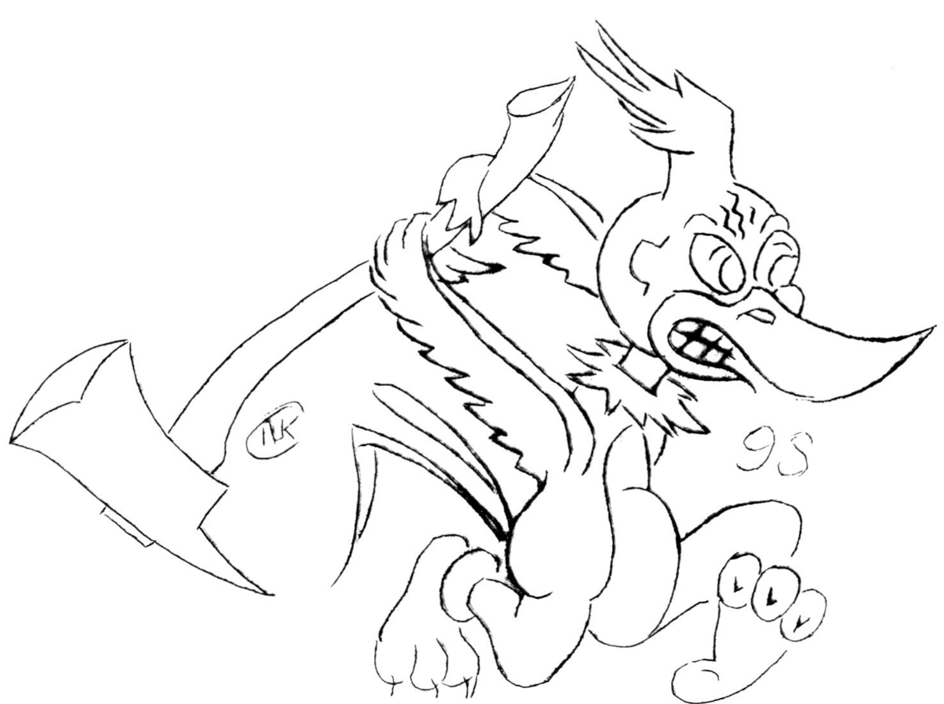

Introduction

The acetate stencil is rarely used today but was used by tattoo artists for decades. They are now a treasured collectible, all thanks to Kate Hellenbrand. I warmly call her The Stencil Queen.

Kate was the first person to display and market her collection of Sailor Jerry acetate stencils at tattoo conventions around the country. Her enthusiasm for this lost art is contagious. This new facet of tattoo collectible immediately captured the imagination of tattoo memorabilia collectors, in and out of the tattoo community.

For over 80 years, the tattoo artist transferred their images onto the skin using clear plastic stencils. (I use the term "plastic" as any man-made synthetic material, preferably transparent, that comes in sheets and can be etched.)

During the tattoo process, the skin must be held taut and stretched in different directions to properly impregnate the pigments into the skin. An image must be transferred onto the skin of the client to maintain a design's proportion and shape. Without an image placed on the skin to work by, the tattoo could easily be distorted and out of proportion.

Many stenciling methods have been employed to transfer images onto the skin. Before plastic, woodblock and paper transfers were the most popular.

Stenciling with a woodblock is probably the earliest method and was used the most worldwide. Woodblock stencil designs were carved into wood. This was time-consuming and the stencils were bulky to carry and store. Paper stencils were made by drawing the design on paper with hectograph ink and then transferring the design onto the skin. This made for a short stencil life and they had to be redrawn often.

As soon as sheet plastic was introduced, tattoo artists around the world adopted it as the preferred stenciling medium. It was easy to find, easy to store and transport and easy to use. Acetate was the preferred plastic. Other compounds were highly flammable, would easily discolor, would curl and not stay flat or would give out an unpleasant odor.

The birth of this type of stencil dates back to the first decade of the last century with the introduction of plastic. The oldest stencils I have documented in my Tattoo Art Museum are ones that are actually scribed on celluloid shirt collars.

Tattooing using a plastic stencil is different than using a modern stencil. Where you start and the direction in which you tattoo the design become important factors. To the untrained eye, an acetate stencil can look like just a crude sketch on a piece of plastic. But to the trained tattoo artist, just a few lines can speak volumes. With a complicated design, the economy of lines is important to prevent confusion. The simple lines of an acetate stencil are more like landmarks that tell the artist where to shade and what to outline. Each artist has his or her own technique when making their stencils — their own code that tells them how to complete the tattoo. (A simple triangle can end up being a row of feathers on an eagle.)

With clear plastic a tattoo artist could easily make a stencil that would last for thousands of impressions. First they would cut the plastic to the size of the design and tape it over a drawing. Then, using a pointed object, often an electric scribing machine, the tattoo artist would etch the basic rudiments of the design into the plastic. The purpose of the stencil has always been to be a guide, not a finished piece of art.

For most collectors the most valuable prize is a collectible that is new and still in the box. But to me, the most beautiful tattoo acetate is the one that has been on a thousand arms. When I look at an acetate with the pigment still in the lines, I think of the thousands of sailors, on their first leave or on their way to war, who stopped at my shop to mark that moment in time into their skin for life.

The designs on acetate stencils clearly show the thoughts of the time and the kind of patrons that put them on their bodies. From bulldogs to mermaids, battleships to devils, the iconography of the acetate stencil shows what was in the hearts of men. Each design represents a symbol to motivate or reminisce, to honor or give homage . . . or to guide and protect.

This Sailor Jerry acetate collection is one of the largest and best kept collection of any one tattoo artist. It marks a time of a fine craft, a time in a tattooist's life, a time in history.

I hope you enjoy and appreciate the following pages as much as I do. For me, they are a walk down memory lane.

Lyle Tuttle
Tattoo Artist/Historian

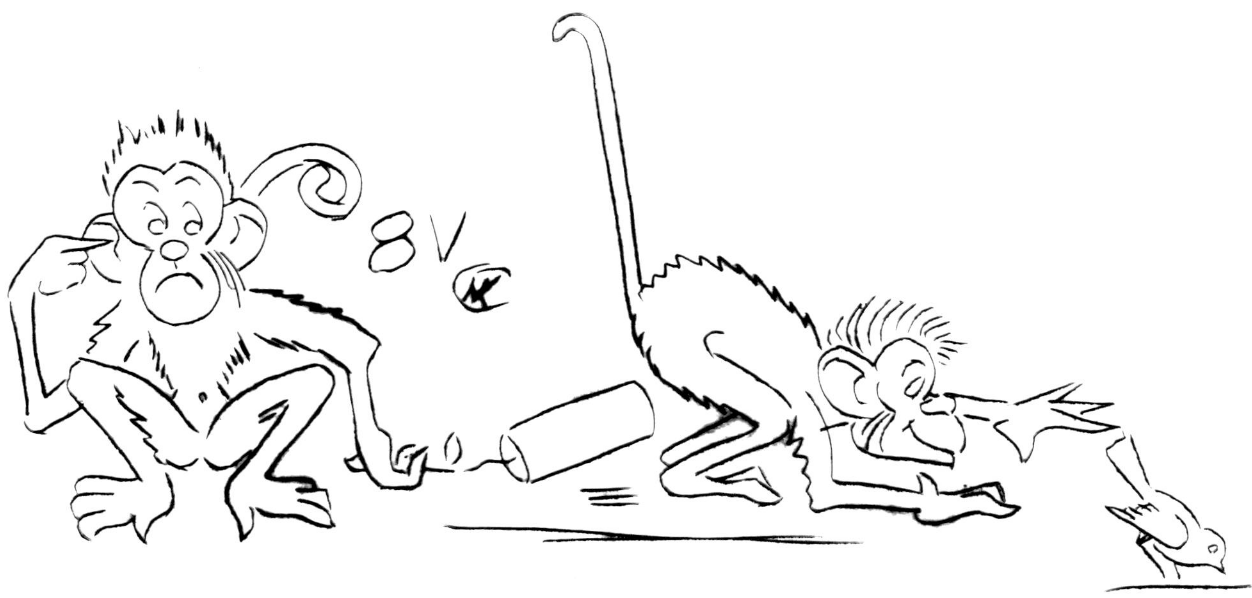

As Old as Time, as Modern as Tomorrow . . . What Is a Tattoo?

"A tattoo is an artificial pigmentation of the skin performed by a prick with a needle."
Sailor Jerry, 1973

Describing the art of tattooing is like trying to nail a cloud to a wall. The process looks simple enough: put a needle in a tube, secure it into the door-bell buzzer-like machine, dip the tip in color . . . and go!

Many hapless newcomers have been seduced by the seemingly simplistic tools.

But what happens if the machine doesn't "go?" How do you know which basic element went awry? Suddenly, the procedure of putting a line of black ink into a human body and having it stay is an enigmatic conundrum of skin types, electronic wizardry, chemical processes, metallurgic properties, medical dangers and more.

These simple elements defy simple explanation.

It takes a lifetime to learn how to tattoo well and the best way to shortcut the arduous process is to apprentice one's self to an accomplished master. The trouble is: master tattoo artists seldom take unskilled apprentices these days. And in the past it wasn't easier or more common.

Sailor Jerry struggled with writing a book (as yet unpublished) explaining his views on the art. (Old-school tattoo artists were also loath to disclose any "secrets" or information more meaty than anecdotal tidbits partly due to fear of lost income, but also out of respect for a hierarchy that demanded only those who had "earned the right to know" should be given the chance to learn.) Sadly, unknown numbers of stories and techniques have passed on with their keepers.

One thing is known, however. Tattooing has been a worldwide phenomenon for possibly tens of thousands of years. When Charles Darwin, author of the theory of evolution, spent a decade investigating our planet in the greatest scientific expedition to his time, he and his team were stunned to discover that wherever they went — no matter how far-flung or remote — the peoples they encountered all engaged in ritualistic body modification. Sometimes the societies employed piercing or scarification or stretching or restrictive practices, but whenever possible, tattooing was most often used by these groups to denote class, maturity or acquisition of power within their group. In trying to describe tattooing's remarkable and universal appeal, Darwin wrote in his journal of the voyages, *Descent of Man* (1871, page 327):

> *"It is extremely improbable that these practices, which are followed by so many distinct nations, are due to a tradition from any common source. They rather indicate the close similarity of the mind of man, to whatever race he may belong, in the same manner as the almost universal habits of dancing, masquerading and making rude pictures."*

In other words, Darwin believed, based on his findings, that tattooing was as much a part of the human condition as singing, dancing, dressing up for Halloween or weddings, or tagging graffiti onto a subway car.

Tattooing has been called the oldest art, predating cave and pottery decoration. We have evidence, such as recovered tattooed mummies, frozen tattooed corpses and carbonized tattooing tools, that the practice of tattooing could reach back to when societal groups first began living together in caves. (The first illustrated book, *Anthropometamorphosis,* documenting human oddities and body alterations was published in 1653.)

Tattoos are known to be highly addictive. People joke that artists must put a drug of some sort into the ink to make people want to come back again and again for more. The truth is more sinister than that. Because tattooing is close to singing or dancing or dressing up, because tattooing has existed all over the world for thousands and thousands of years . . . when tattooists put something under the skin, they also expose a sense of self-awareness — powerful stuff when modern life can cause so many of us to feel disconnected. (Nothing feels as good as success, nothing is as tempting or addictive as the "high" one feels when one finally gets a glimpse into an authentic self.)

Tattoo artists are modern-day shamans, able to uncover ancient memories of warrior-like heroism in their clients, whether it be with a small Japanese brush-stroke character or a giant tiger. (Of course, inscribing a tiger on your skin will not transform you into a tiger anymore than bleaching your hair will make you a natural blonde.)

For years the growth of the tattoo business was slow. Reluctance to share secrets of the trade, lengthy master/apprentice relationships, even the public's disdain for this "lowbrow" art kept the growth fairly flat.

Until recently, it was nearly impossible to become a tattoo artist without a fortuitous stroke of good luck. Now anyone can buy a starter kit, grab a friend and grind out bad tattoos.

And tattoo shops are springing up all over the country like mushrooms in a cow pasture after a good rain. It has been named as one of the top five accelerated businesses in America in the past decade.

One of the major reasons for this growth would be the switching from plastic to thermofax stencils.

Acetate stencils (this term could be a misnomer because stencils were also carved in celluloid, vinyl, mylar and other clear sheeting) were sturdy, durable, compatible with multiple impressions, compact, lightweight and easy to store. (However, storing them could be sometimes dangerous. Several tattoo shops have burned to the ground because a box of stencils self-combusted in the attic or basement.)

While the stencils were sturdy, the images they left behind were not. One brush of an errant hand, one hiccup from a misbehaving machine, one good blast from a rotating fan and the stencil's fragile carbon leavings could disappear. In that case, the artist had to know how to complete the design without panicking in front of an already nervous client.

Today the reverse is true. Thermofax stencils are fragile, tissue-thin paper with a gentian violet backing. But they leave behind an indelible image that is difficult to erase.

Some tattoo artists still use acetates, maybe out of reverence for their old-school forefathers; maybe because the transparency of the material allows for better alignment when covering an old or unwanted tattoo. Enough artists still use this type of stencil to warrant supply companies to continue selling the ground charcoal, pin vises and sheets of mylar.

While the modern paper stencils can seem to make tattooing easier, they will not be preserved for future generations.

An important element in the seemingly simple chain of events has been eliminated.

The basic truths of the art remain.

What is Old is New Again . . . Sailor Jerry and His Stencils

"How are stencils used?"

"The plastic stencils used in tattooing are first cleaned thoroughly by immersion in an antiseptic solution as approved by the Hawaii State Department of Health for a period of at least ten minutes and then wiped dry with a sterile gauze sponge. Chemically pure sterile activated charcoal is then sprinkled lightly on the surface of the stencil and rubbed into the etched lines thereof with a piece of dry sterile gauze. Prepared in this fashion, the stencil is then applied to the prepared surface of the skin and pressed lightly down upon it, making certain that all of the etched lines of the stencil leave the charcoal imprint of the design on the skin and that the stencil does not skid sideways to leave a smeared imprint. Your imprint of the design on the skin should be a clean-cut, easily visible print that will adequately guide you in the application of the tattoo outline itself."

Excerpts from a proposed magazine interview with Sailor Jerry, not published.

"Sailor Jerry" Norman Keith Collins was possibly the most accomplished American tattoo master to his time. Inventor, innovator, rogue, true renaissance man . . . he defined his craft into two eras: BSJ and ASJ (before and after Sailor Jerry). He did more for the ancient art of tattoo than any other single person. He searched for (and found) pigments that were safe to use, expanding the tattooist's pallete from the three or four colors previously available to an array as vibrant as the rainbows that arced over his Hawaii home.

He created better power sources, machines and needle configurations that could coax pigments into the skin without trauma.

Most importantly, he spearheaded the introduction of single-service products and hospital-style sterilization into the business to prevent the spread of blood-borne pathogens in tattoo shops.

He fought a legendary and often humorous war with "scab vendors" (tattoo artists of shallow skill and suspect motives).

He set standards of execution and quality that remain the hallmark of the industry.

He was an avid proponent of the art of tattoo and, as a staunch conservative, often rankled his community-at-large with his stern demands for respect. He caused a furor when he doubled his fee from $25 to $50 an hour and celebrated when his angered clients swallowed their pride and returned for more work at his new rates.

He rode his baby-blue Harley Davidson motorcycle with sidecar until his last days.

He pursued his many hobbies to the professional level. He was a radio talk-show host, a master seaman, a dance band saxophonist. He was an innovator, a jokester, a genius. He was not always easy to love but always worth your respect.

The images on the following pages are computer-scanned from actual Sailor Jerry hand-carved acetate stencils used during his work in his shop. They are seen exactly as they exist and have not been altered in any way.

Each stencil carries a Sailor Jerry signature: NKC for his given name, Norman Keith Collins; SJ for Sailor Jerry; his signature stamp or a variation of his signature.

The signatures were placed on the reverse side of the stencil so as not to be inadvertently tattooed onto the client. Other markings on the stencils refer to Jerry's filing systems.

In most cases, only one stencil exists for each design. However, as tattoos should aesthetically face into the front of the body, often a right and left version were cut. Also, old school tattooists always had a sheet of flash "in the works," says Zeke Owen, Sailor Jerry colleague and 45-year-plus tattoo artist. Therefore, some stencils have an older and newer version.

The method of display within these pages coincides with the way tattoo shops present their flash . . . randomly, encouraging the viewer to see all the designs as they come up.

The stencils you see here are for sale. Inquiries can be made to the author at Kate@KateHellenbrand.com

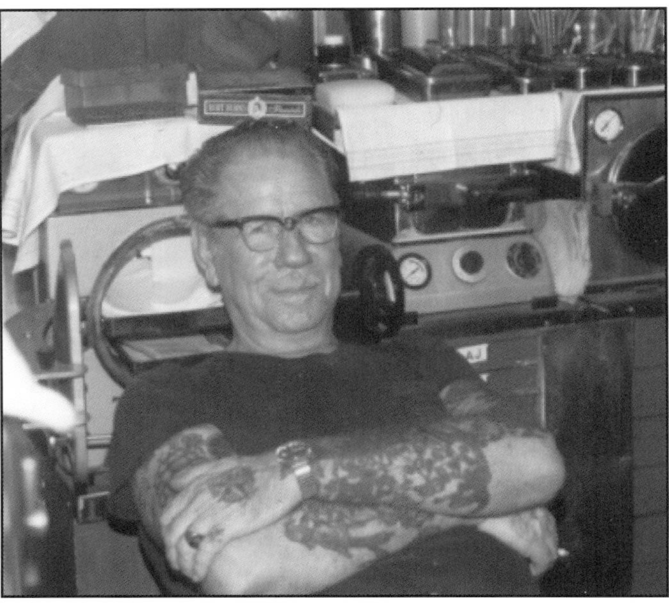

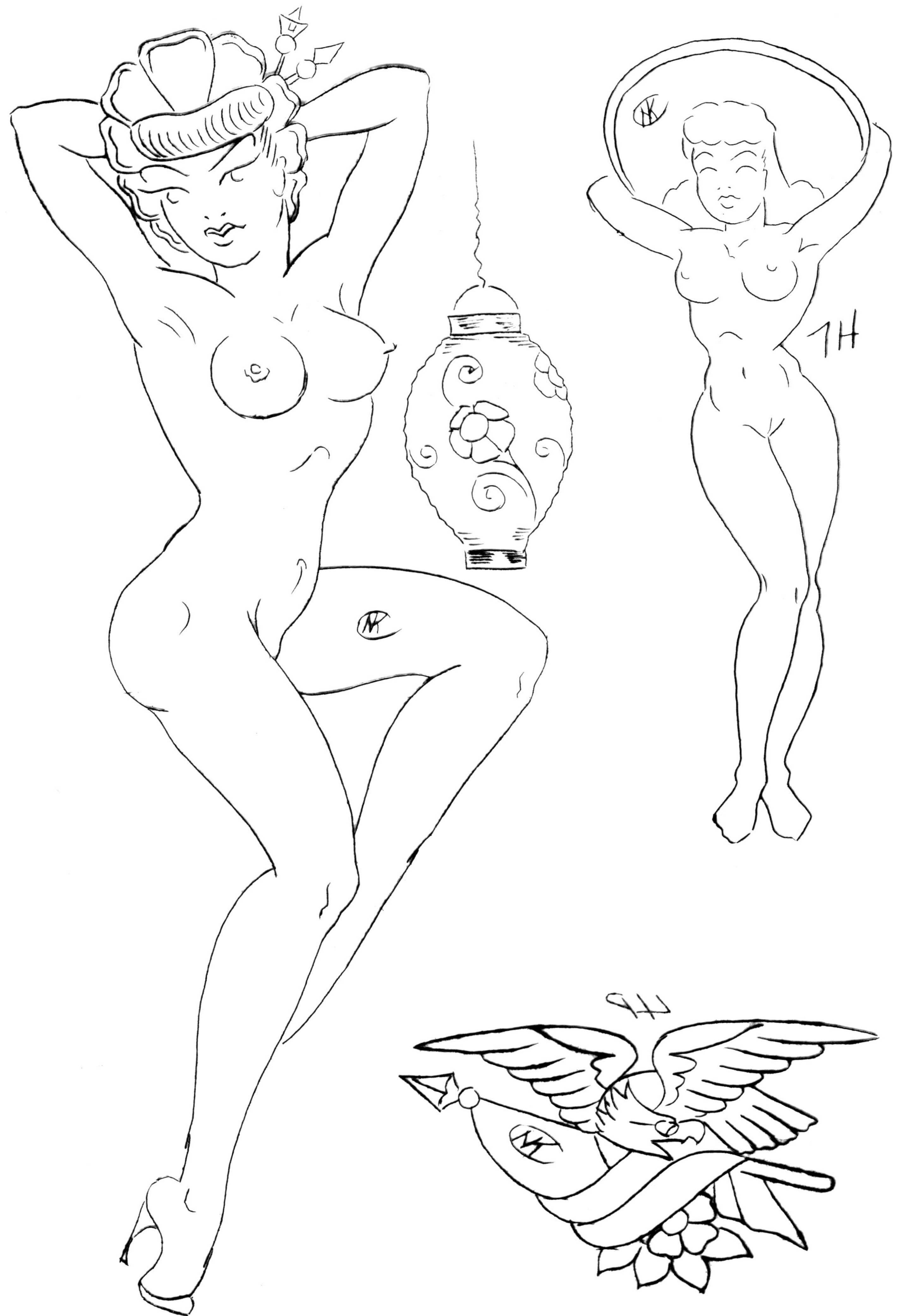

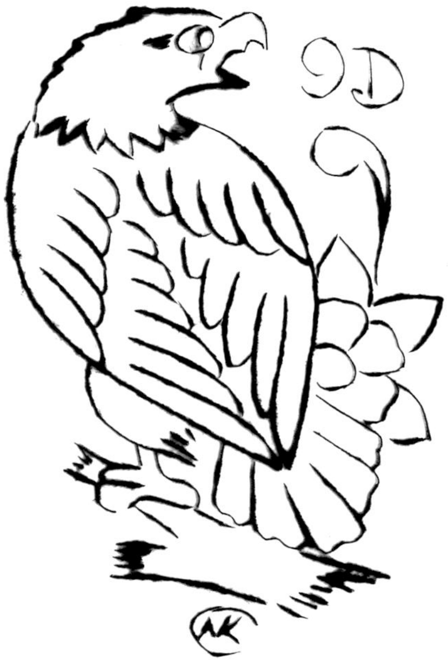

9D

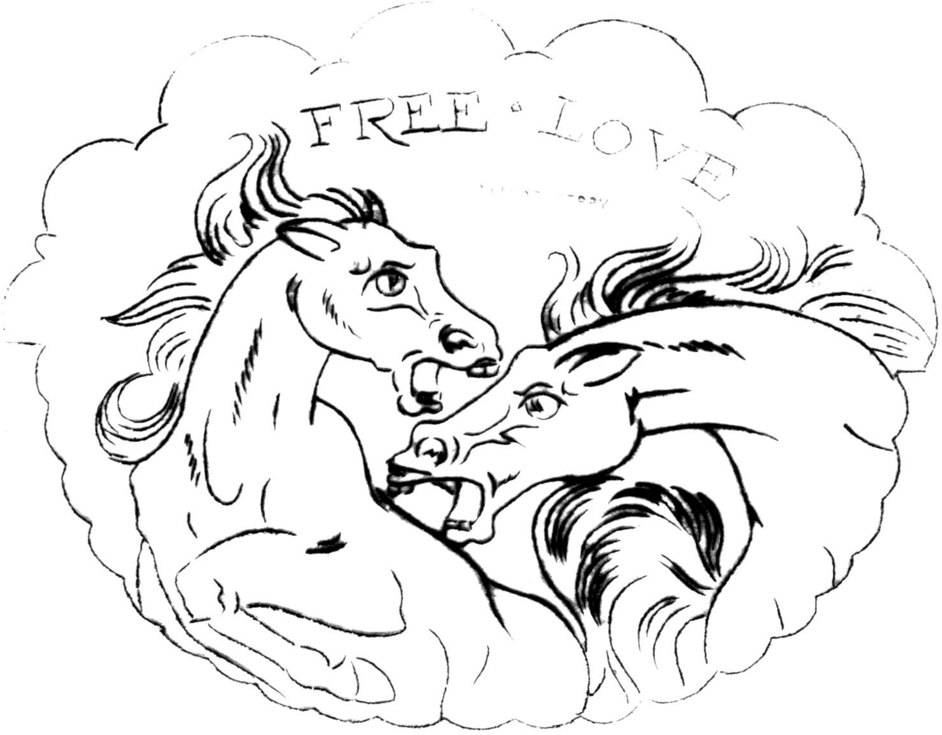

FREE LOVE

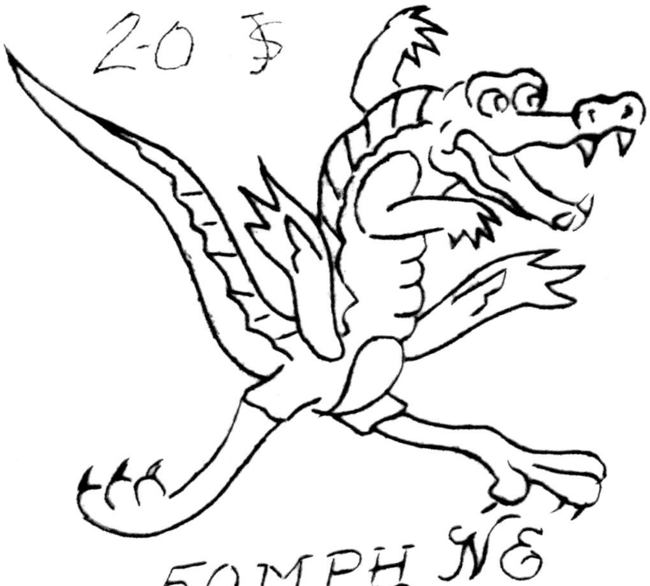

50MPH

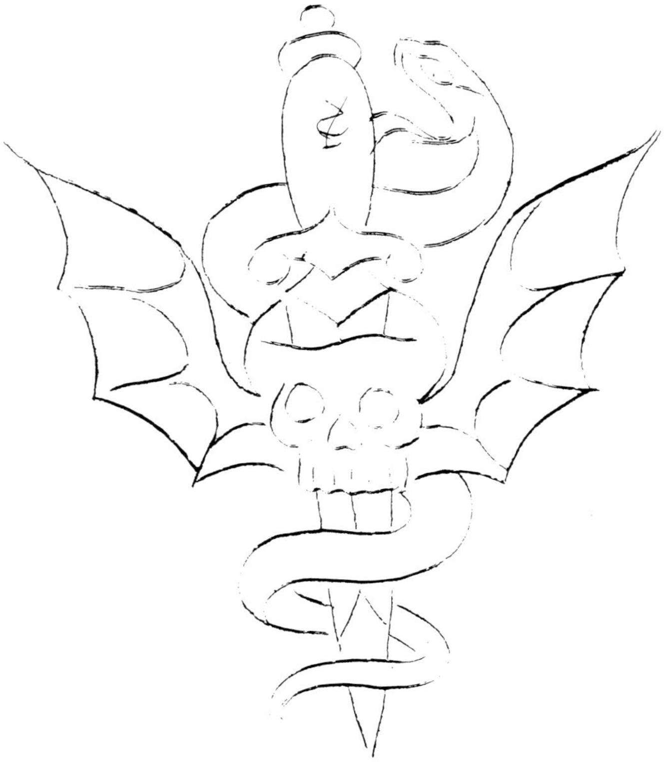

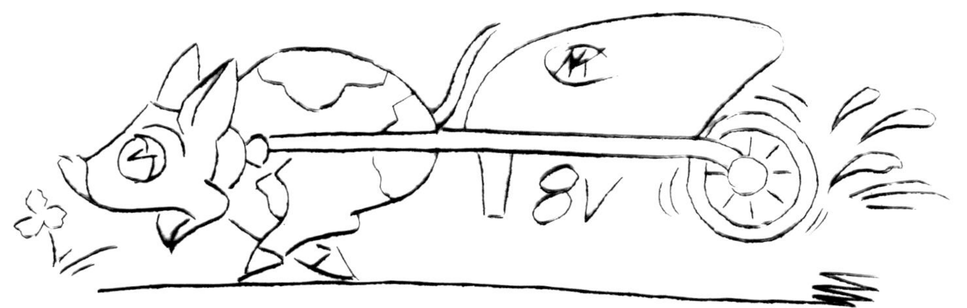

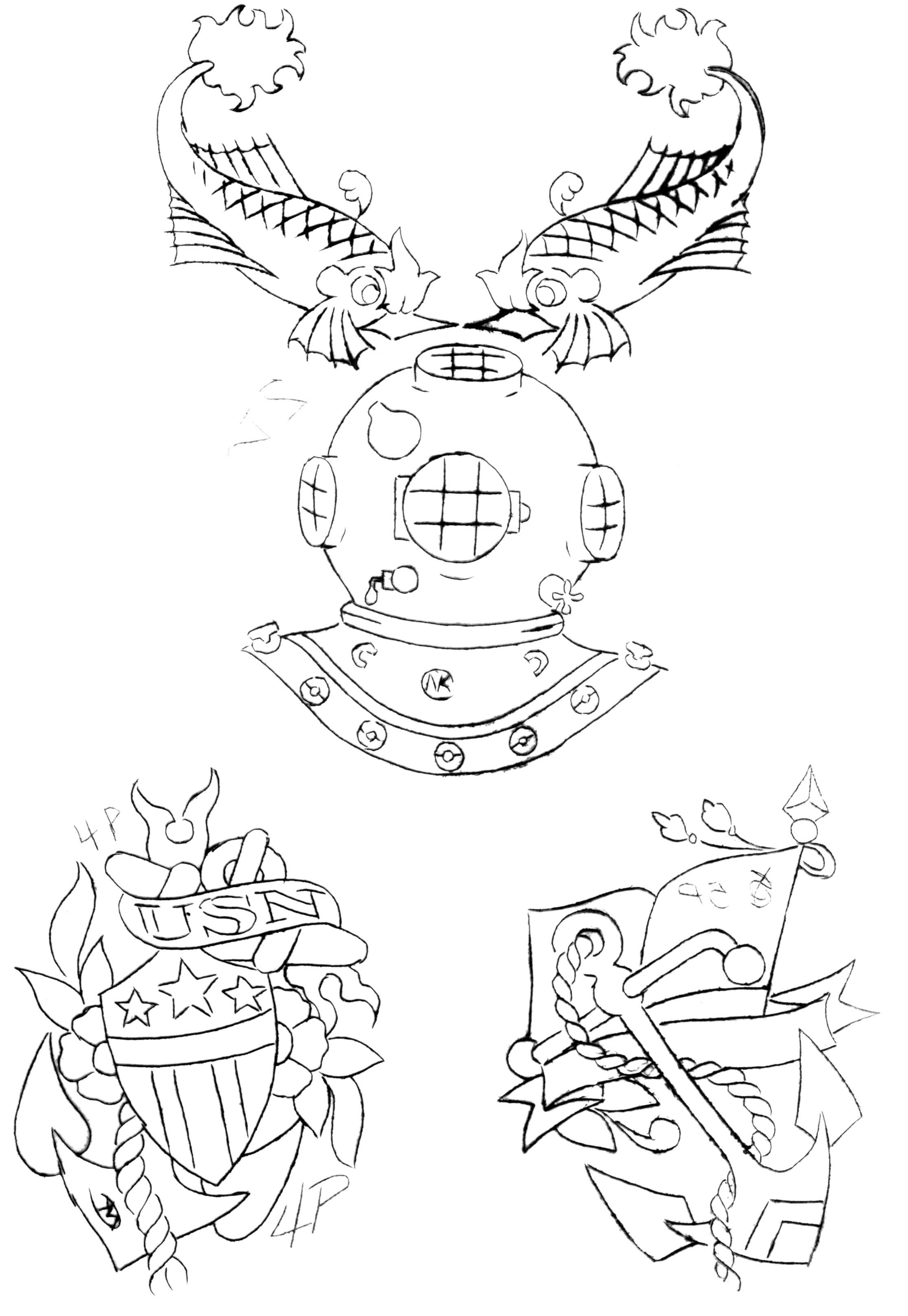

4P
USN
4P

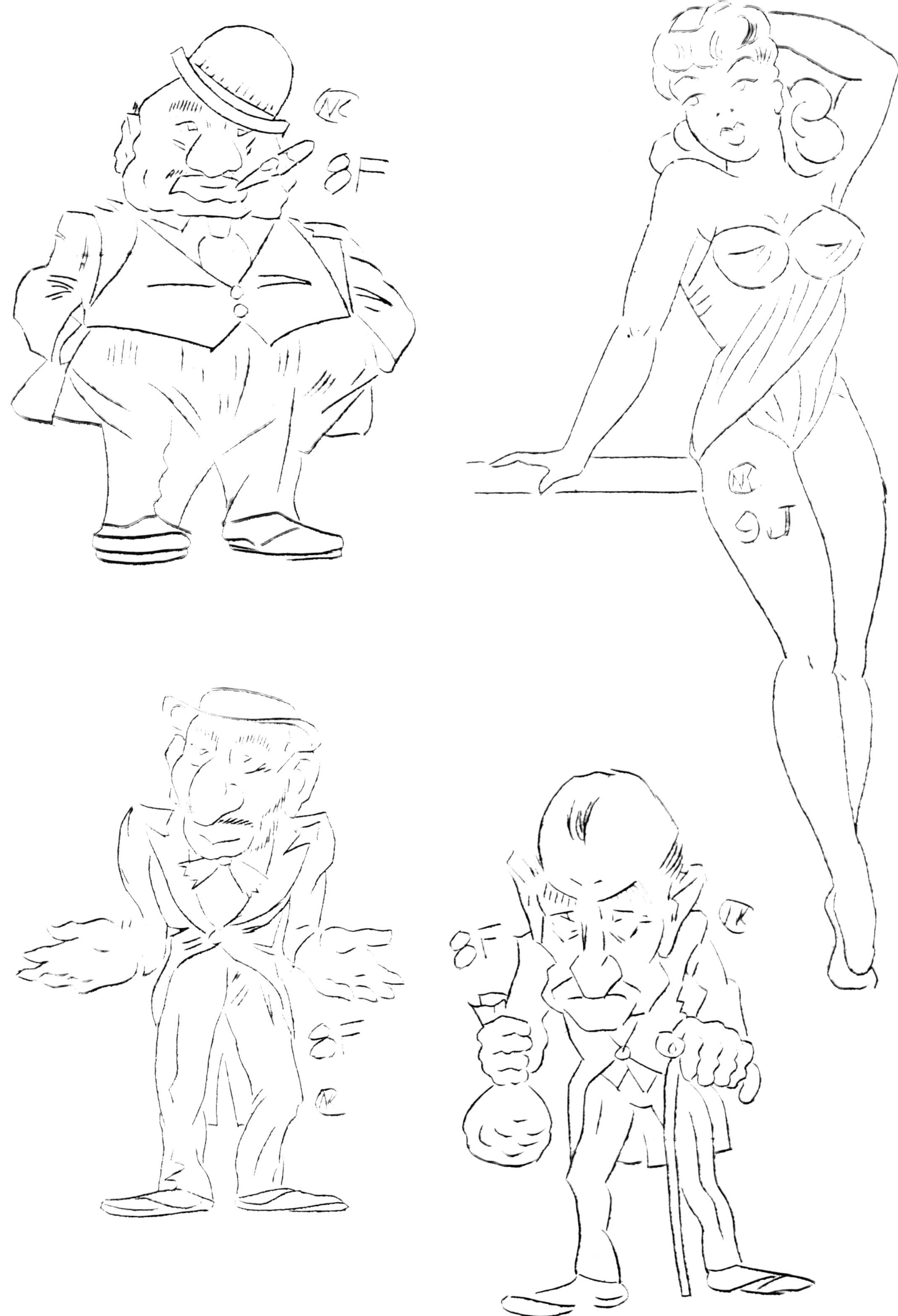
8F
9J
8F
8F

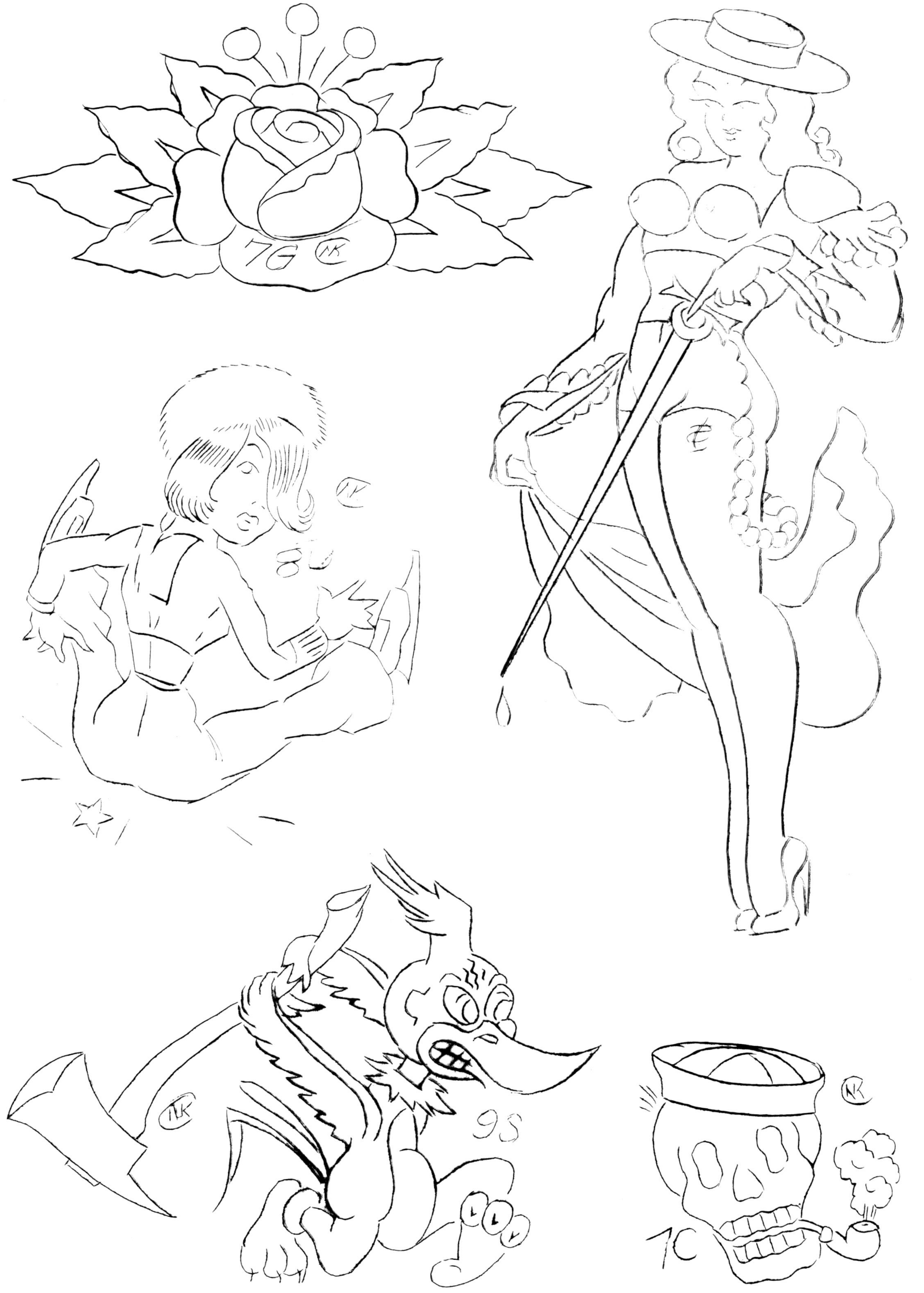

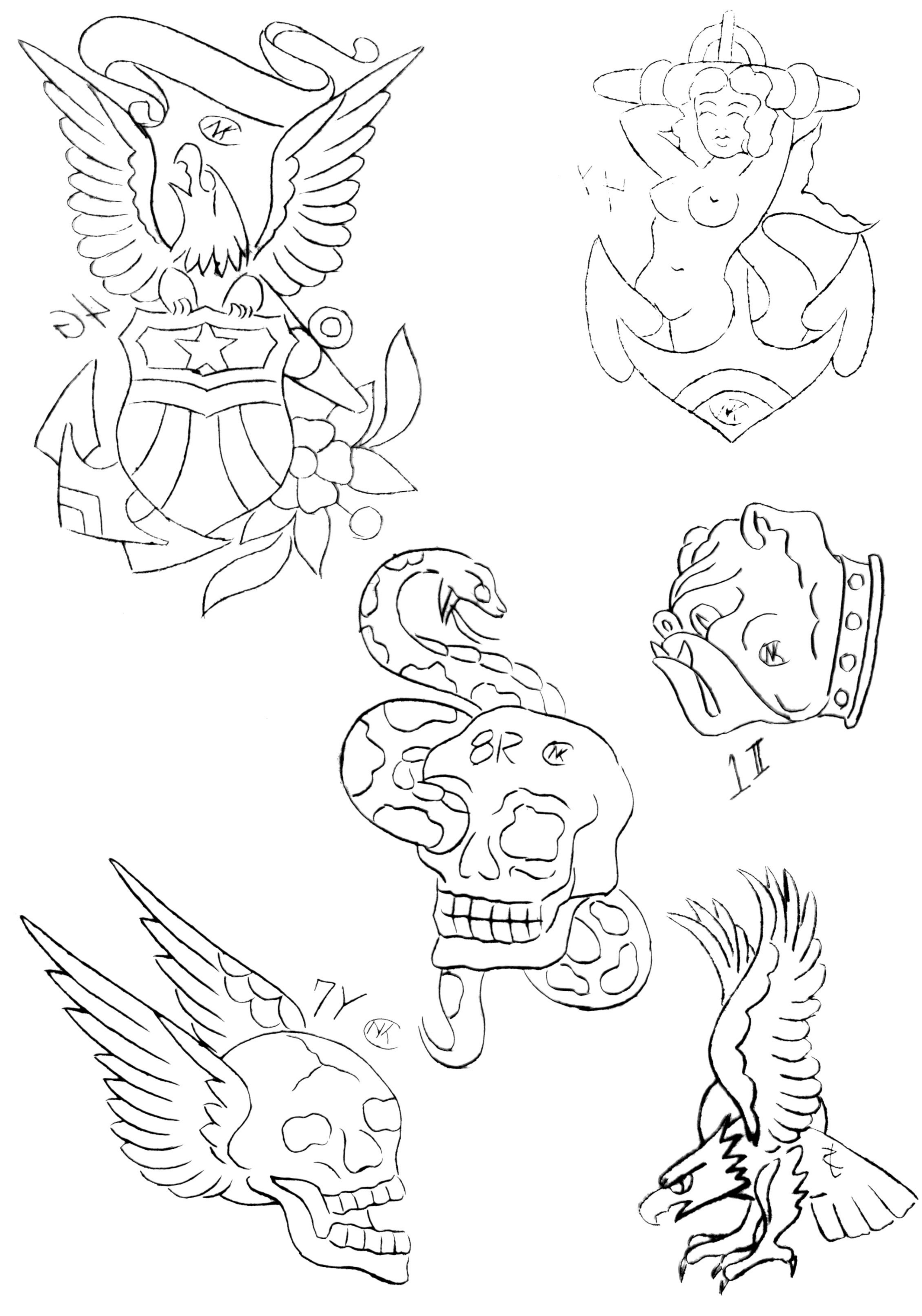
8R
7Y

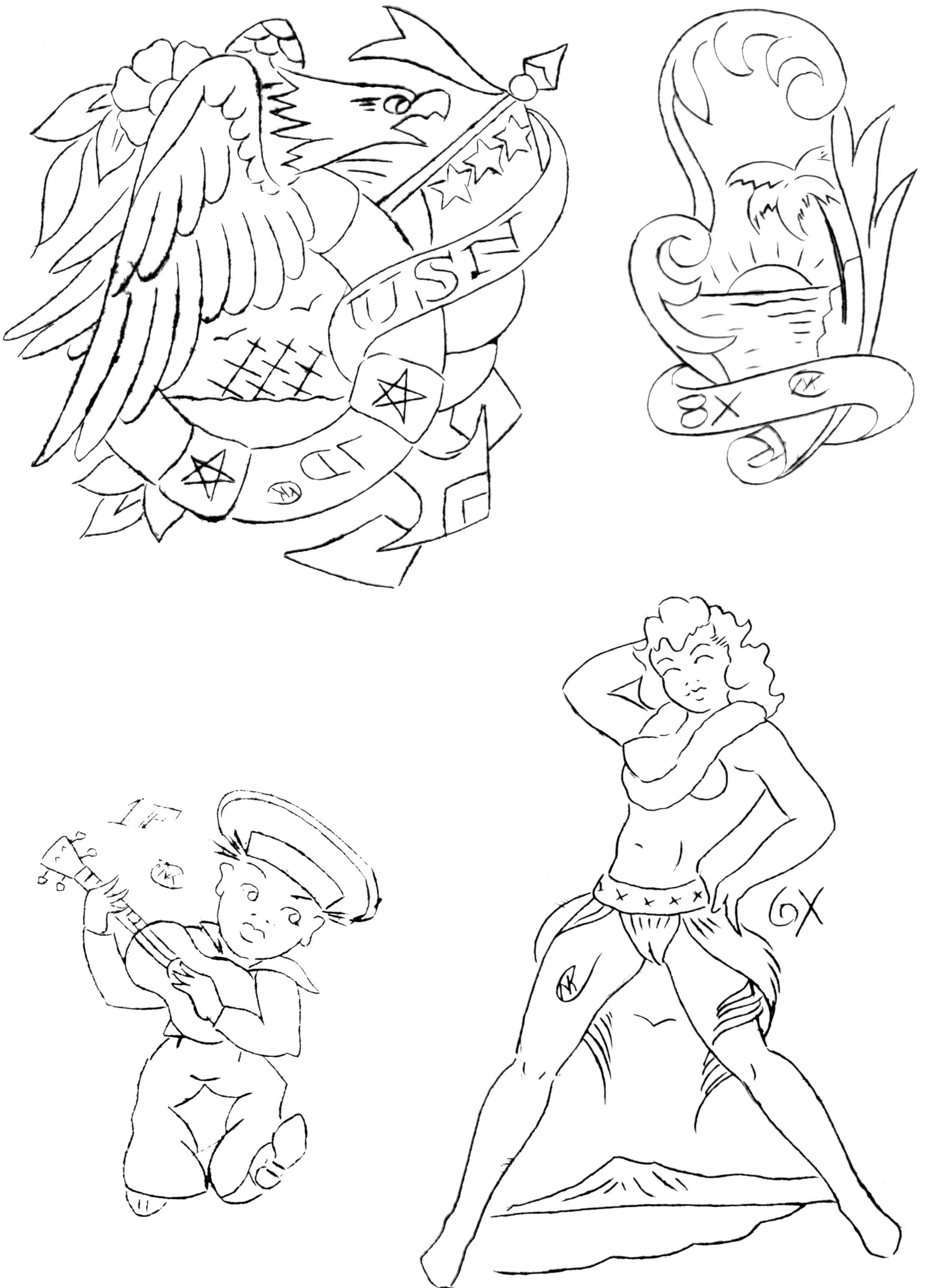
USN
8X
6X

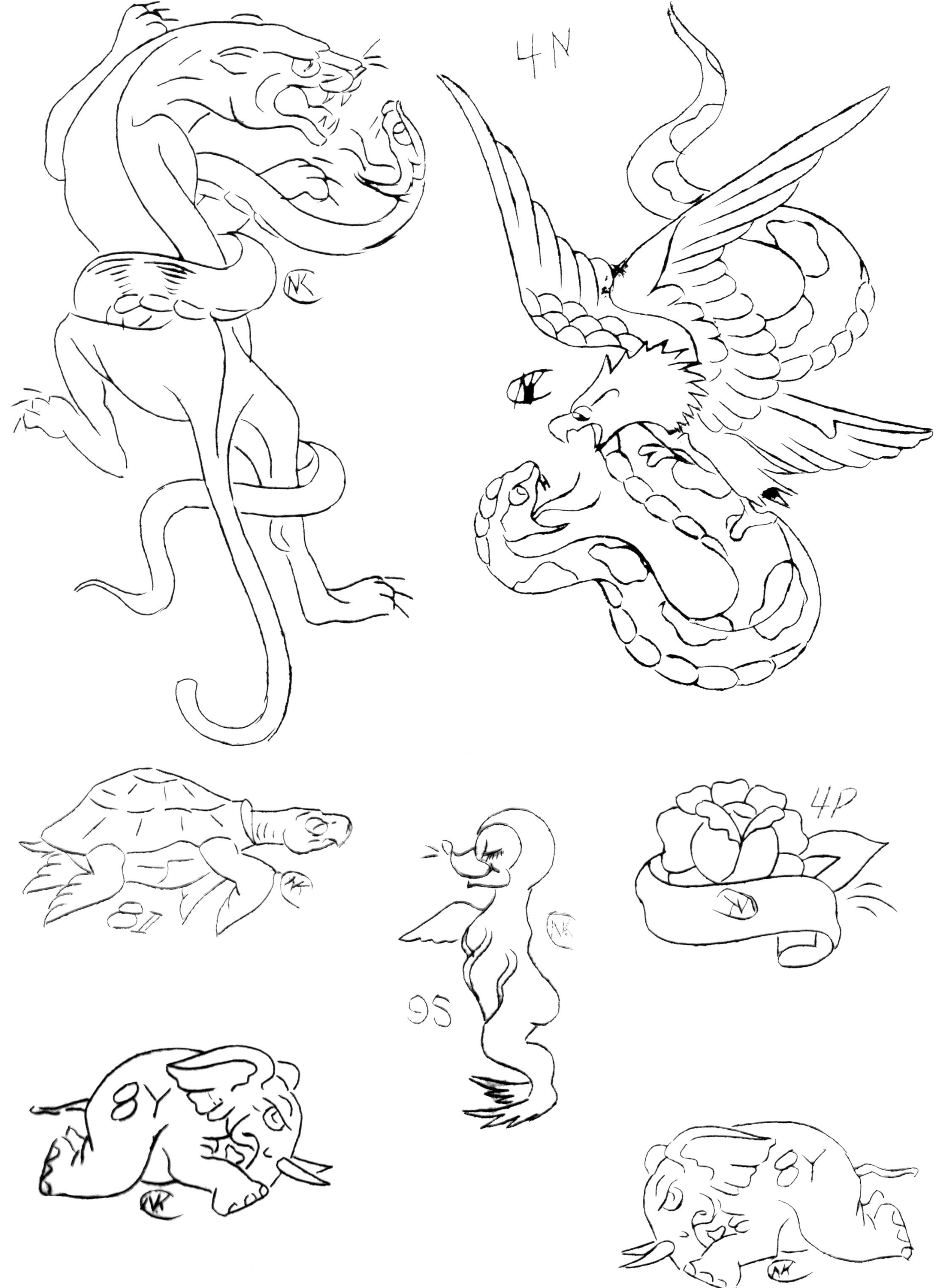
4N
4P
95
8Y
8Y

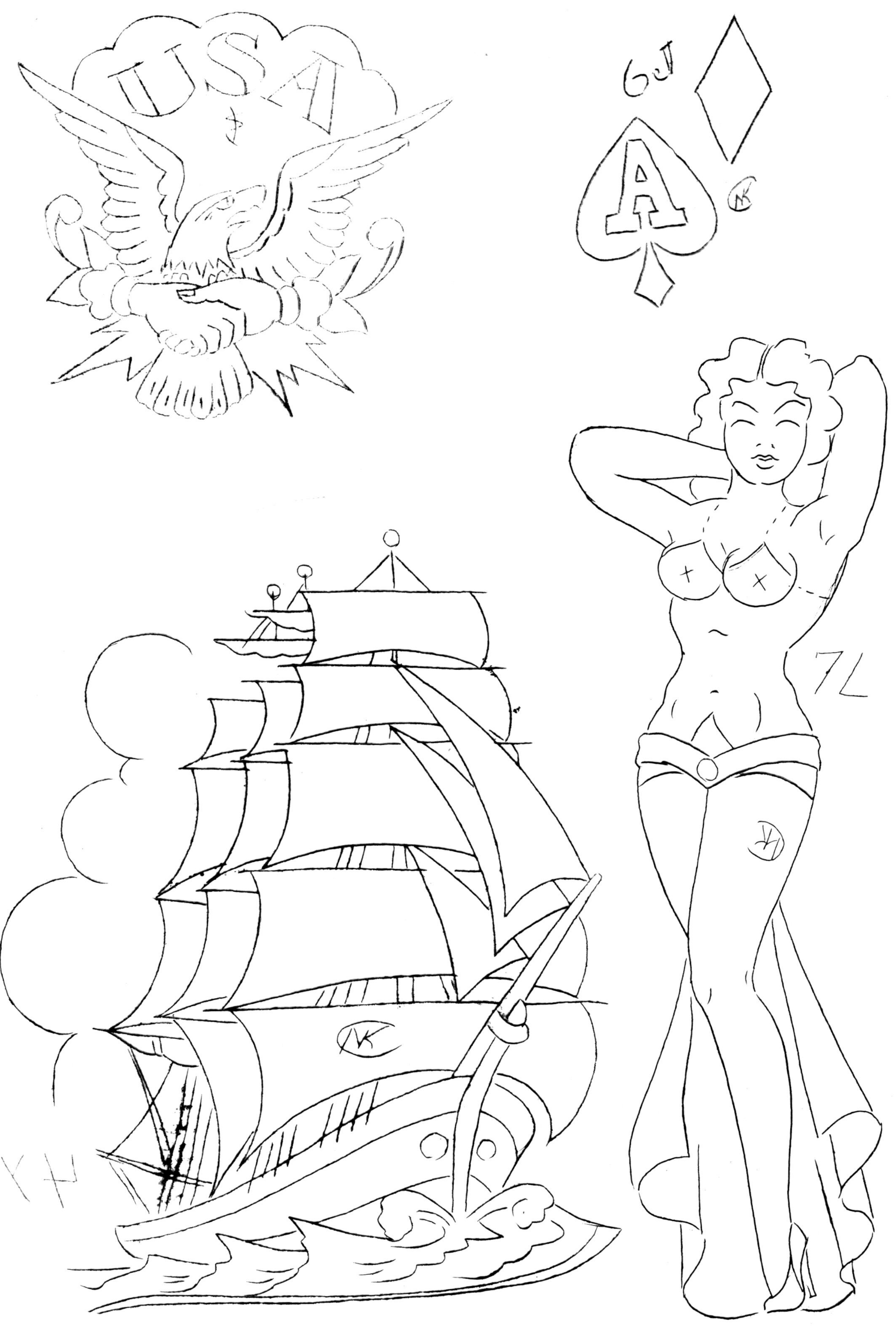
USA
A

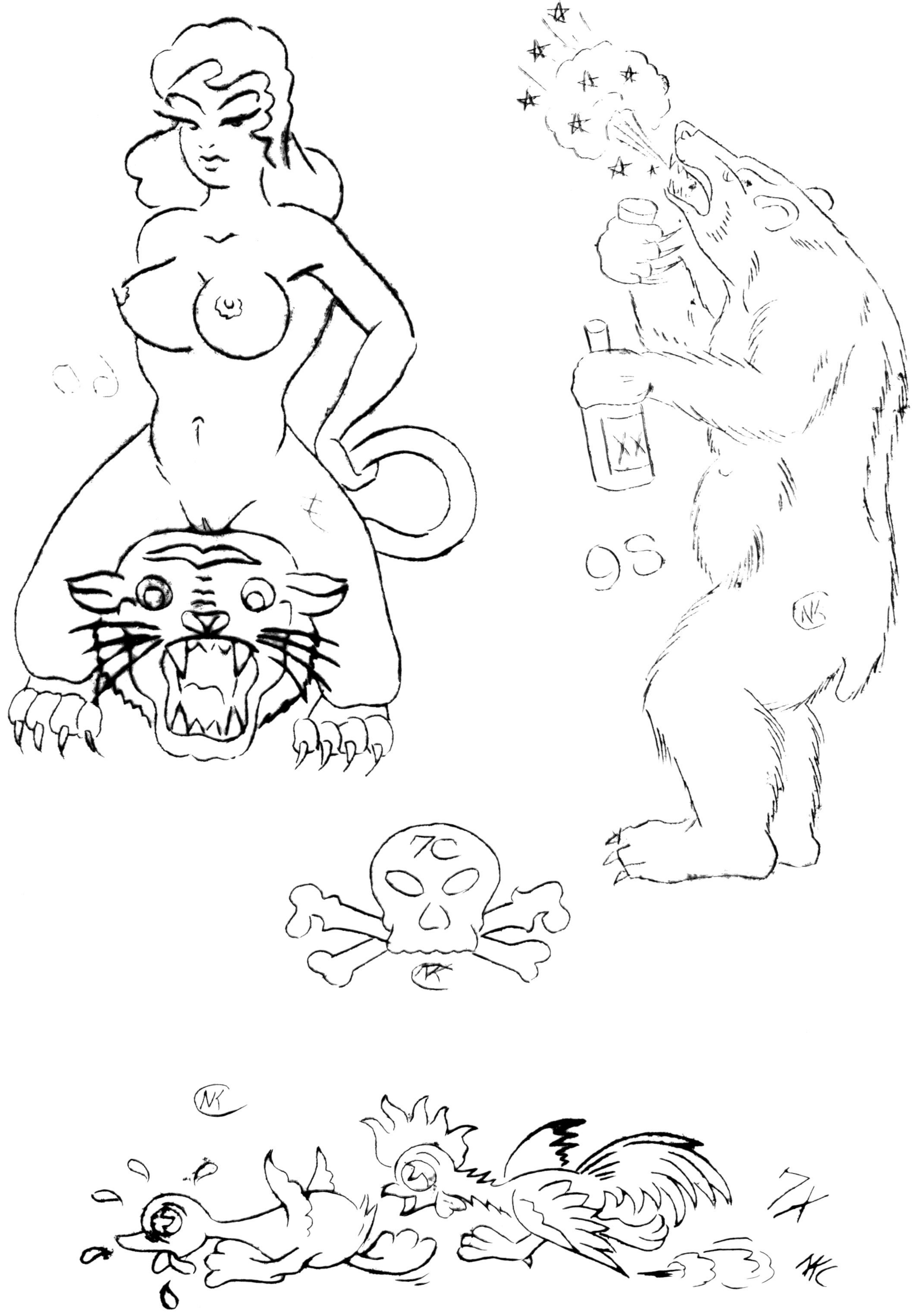

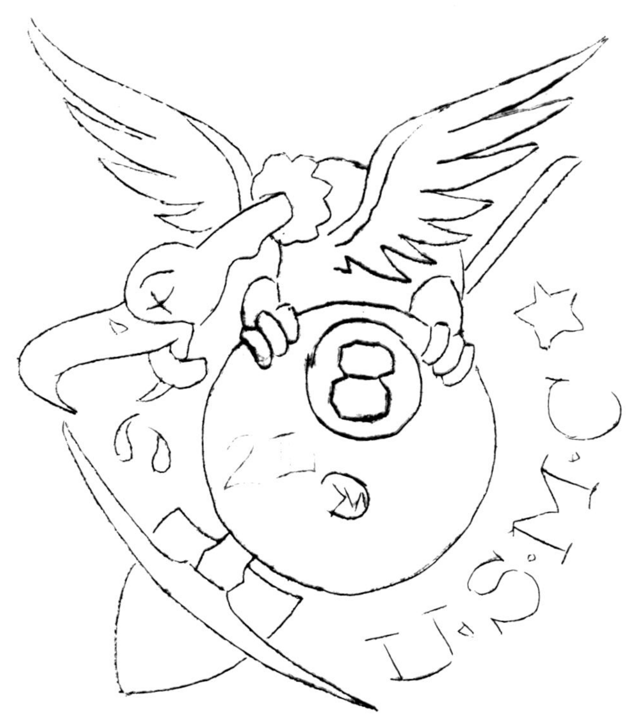
8
U.S.M.C

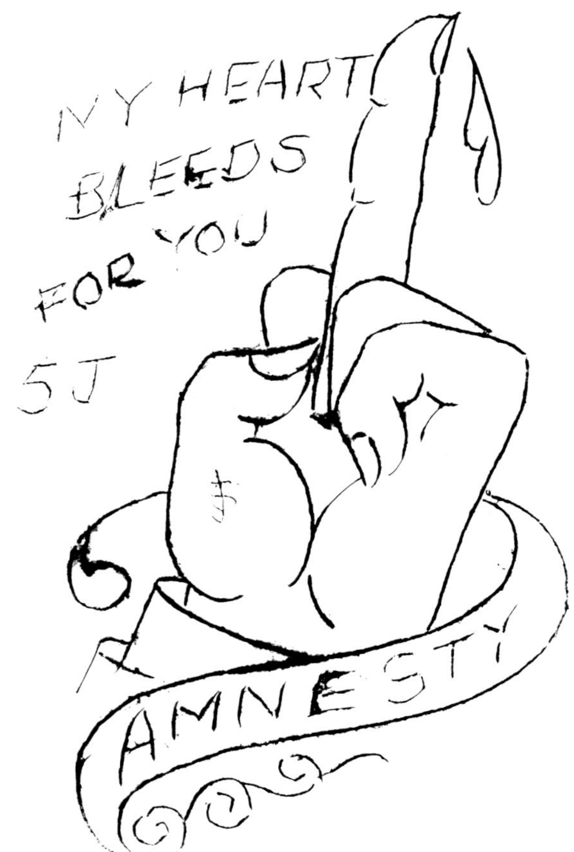
MY HEART
BLEEDS
FOR YOU
5J
AMNESTY

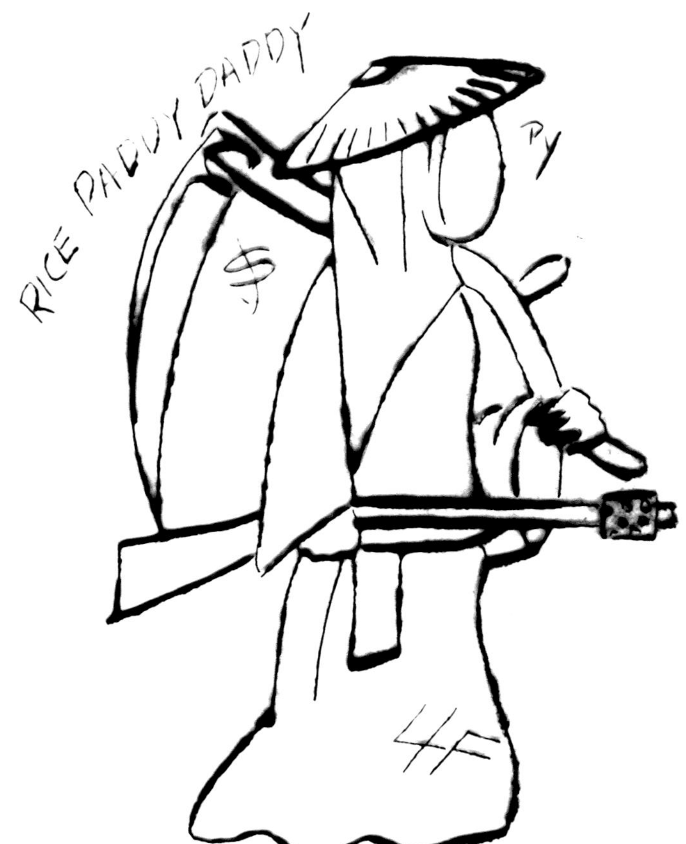
RICE PADDY DADDY

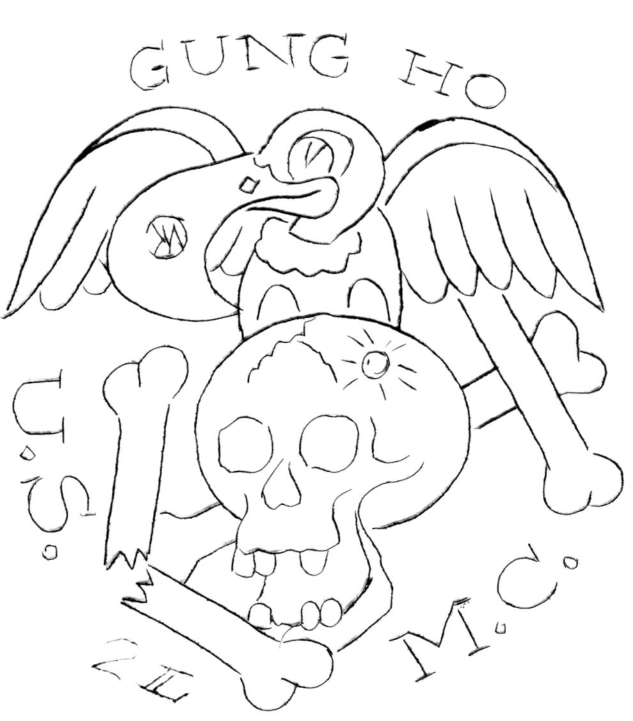
GUNG HO
U.S.
M.C.

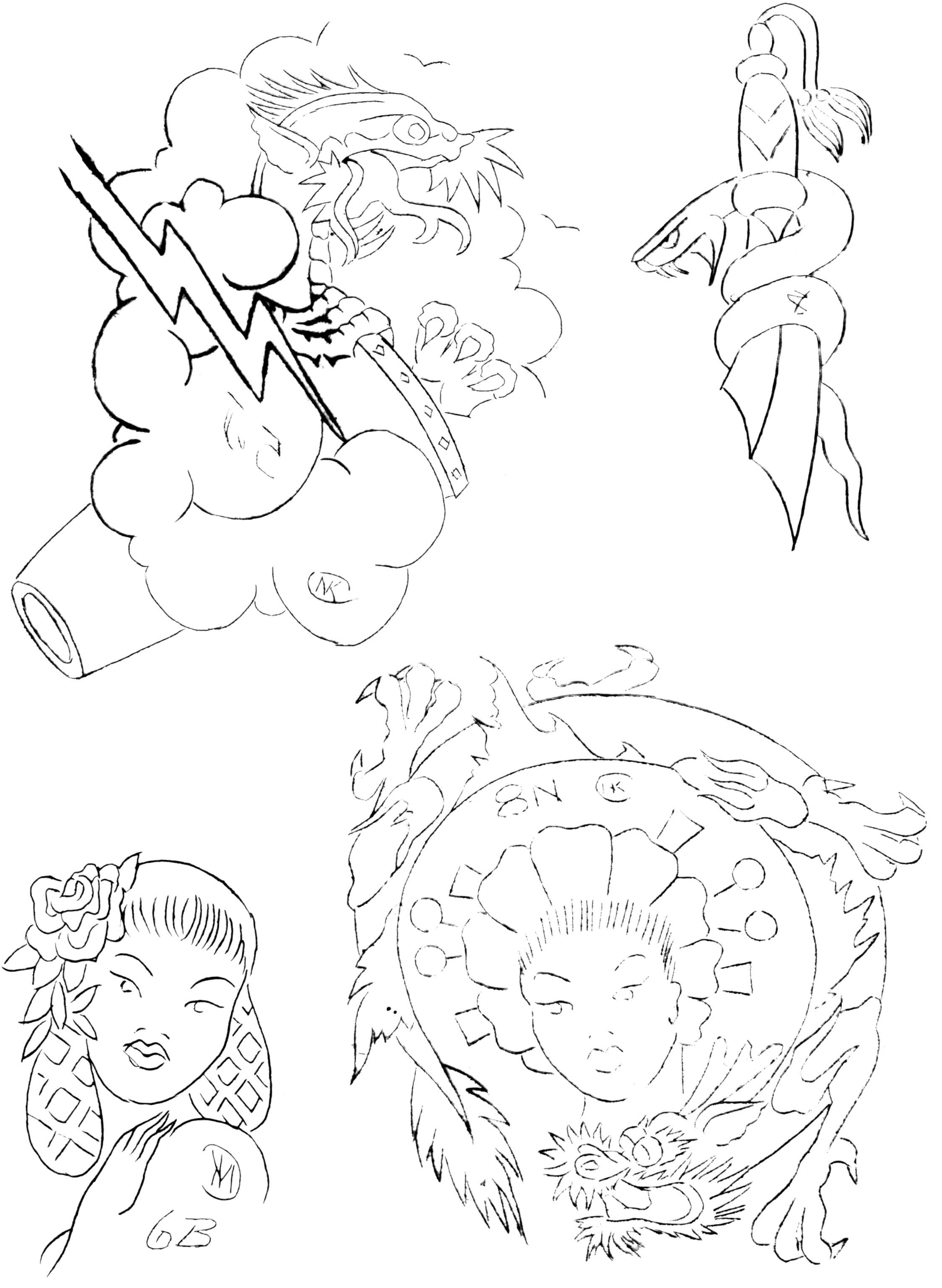
GB

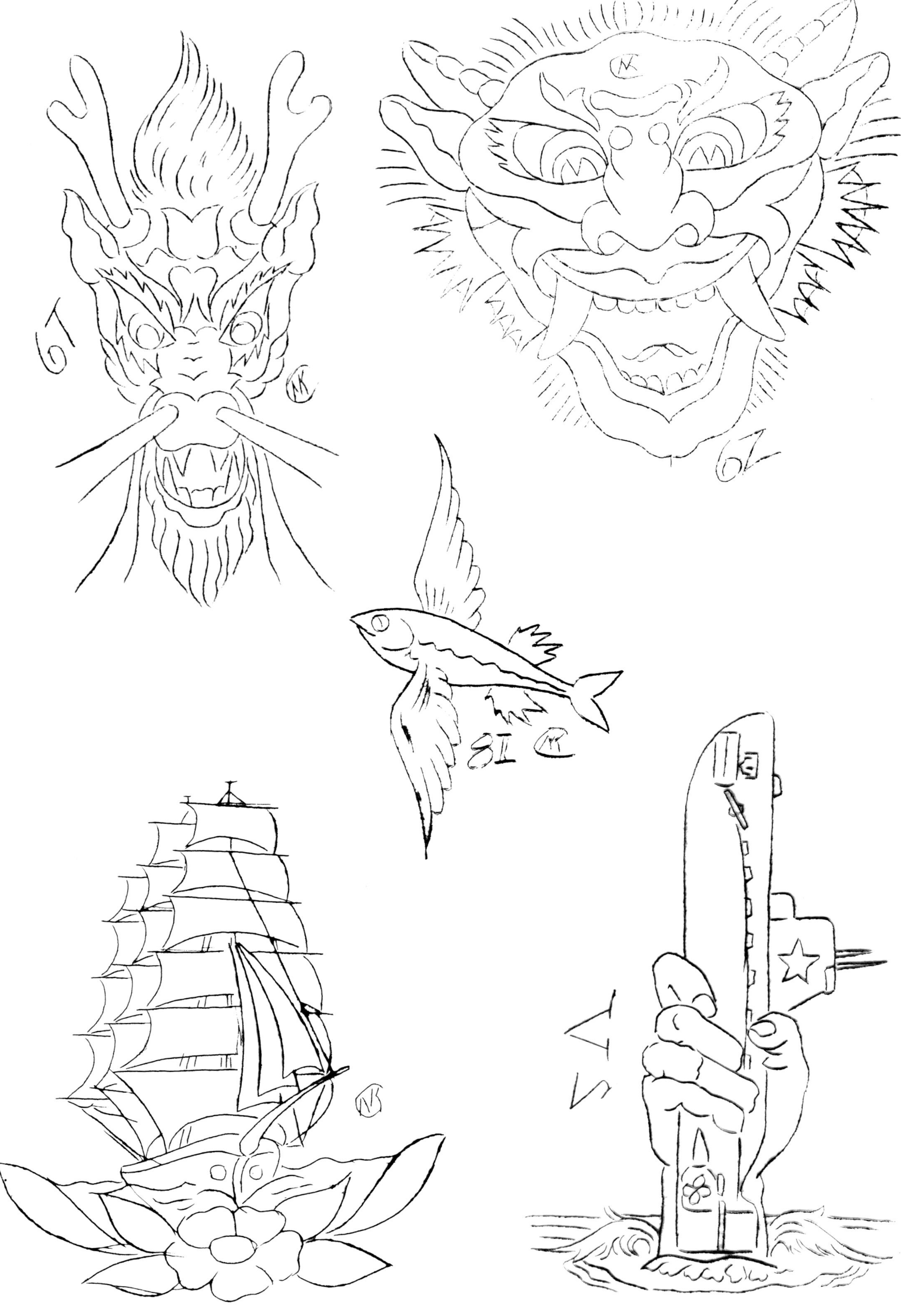

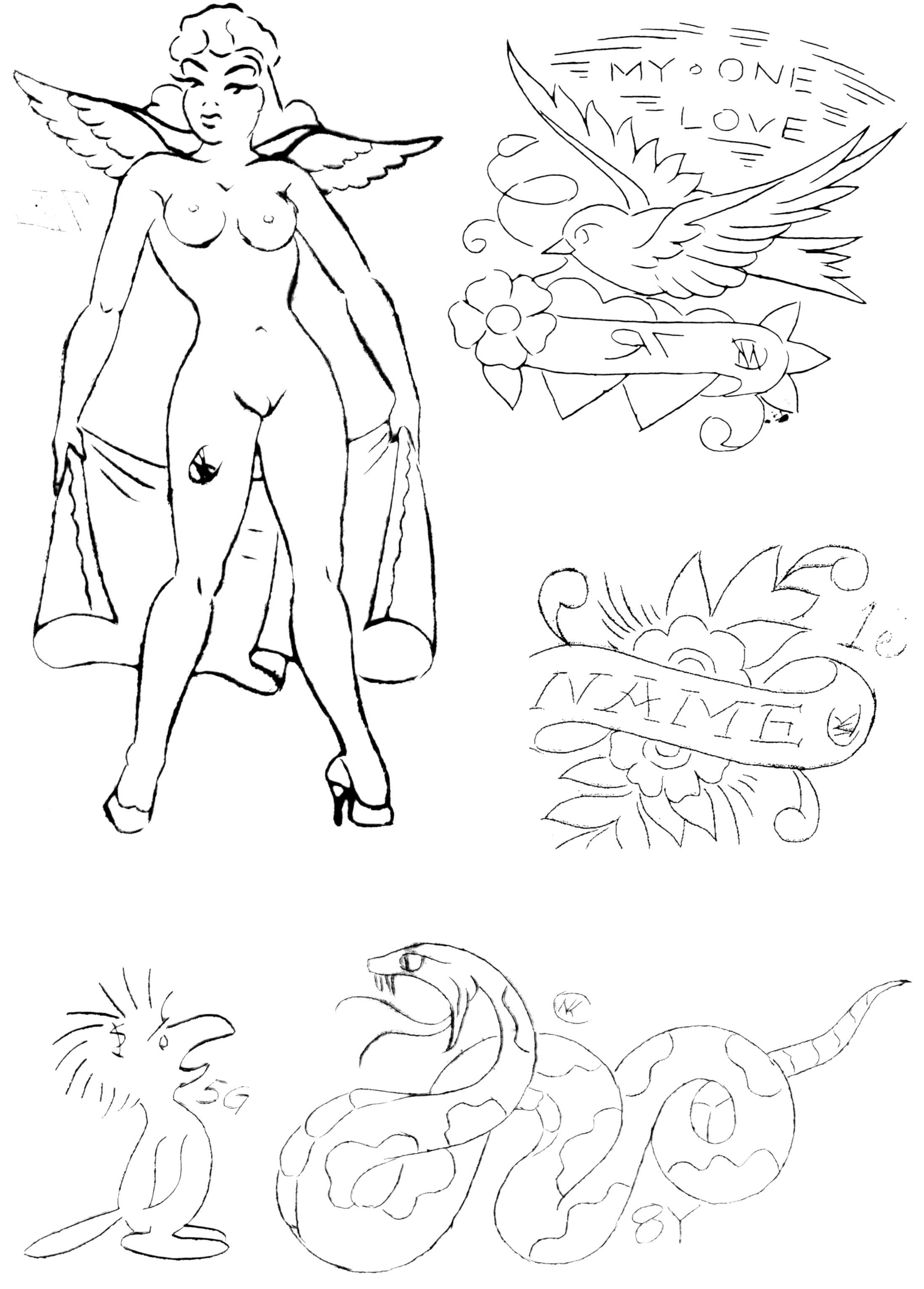
MY ONE LOVE
NAME
5G
8Y

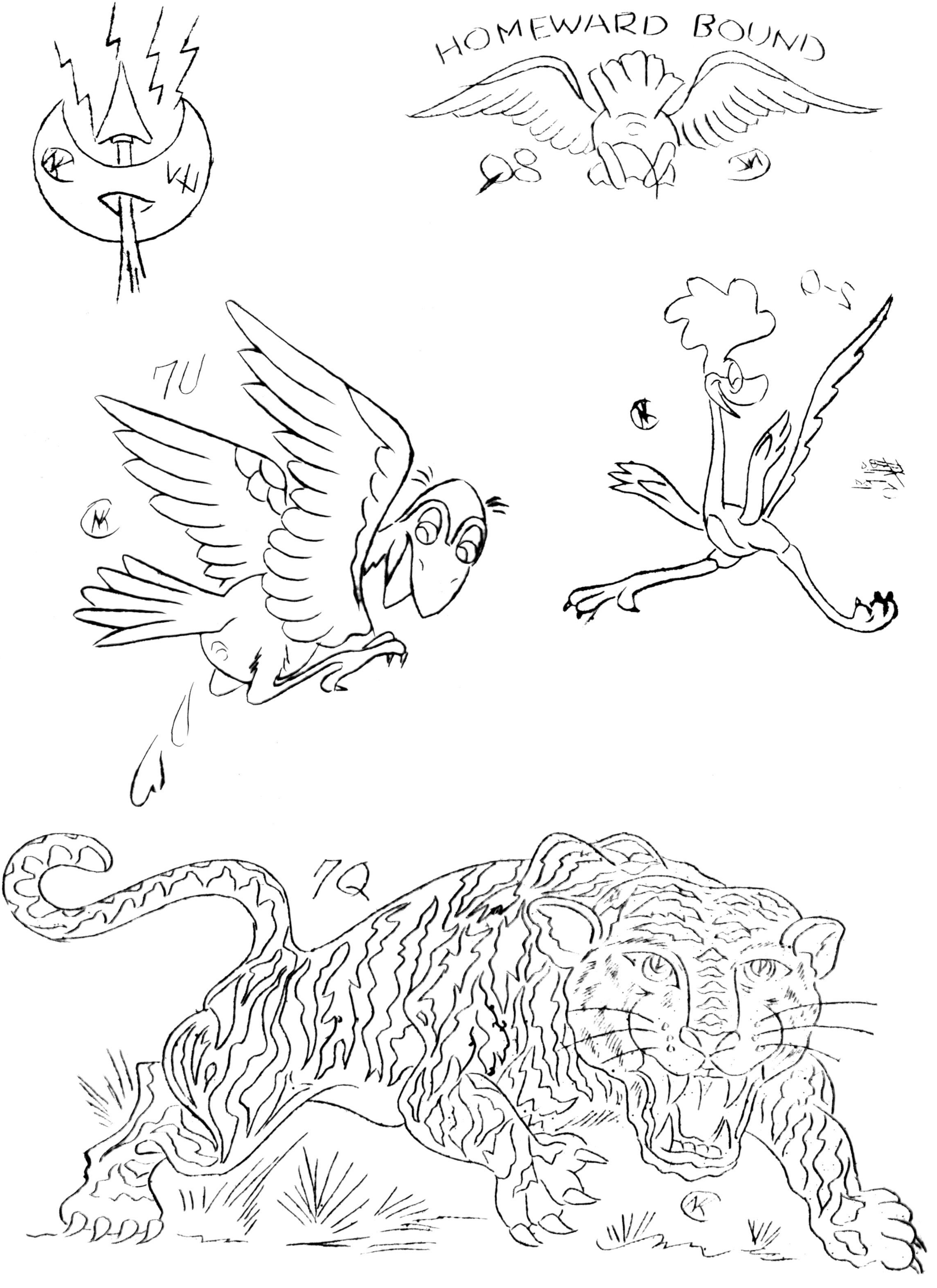
HOMEWARD BOUND
7U
7Q

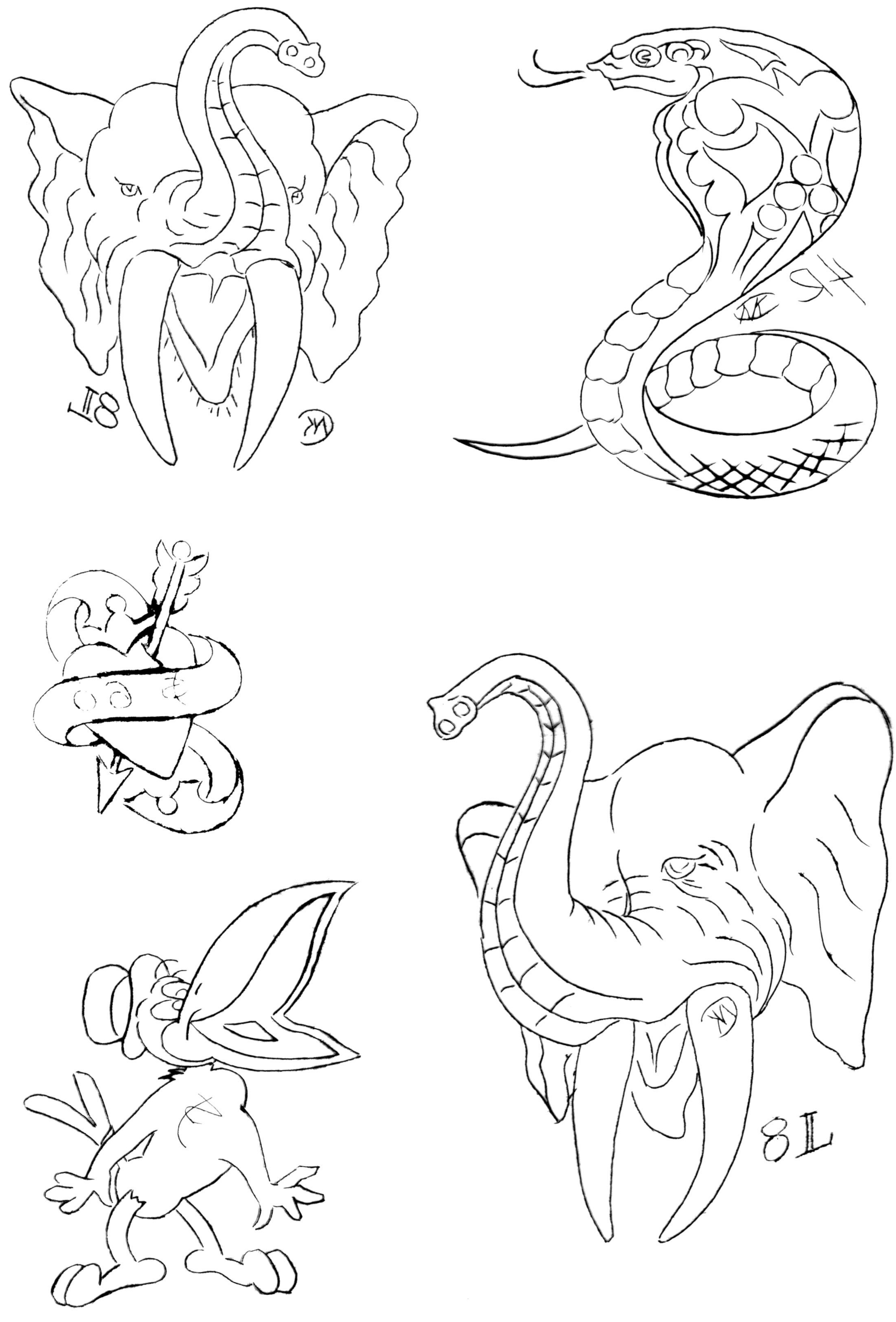

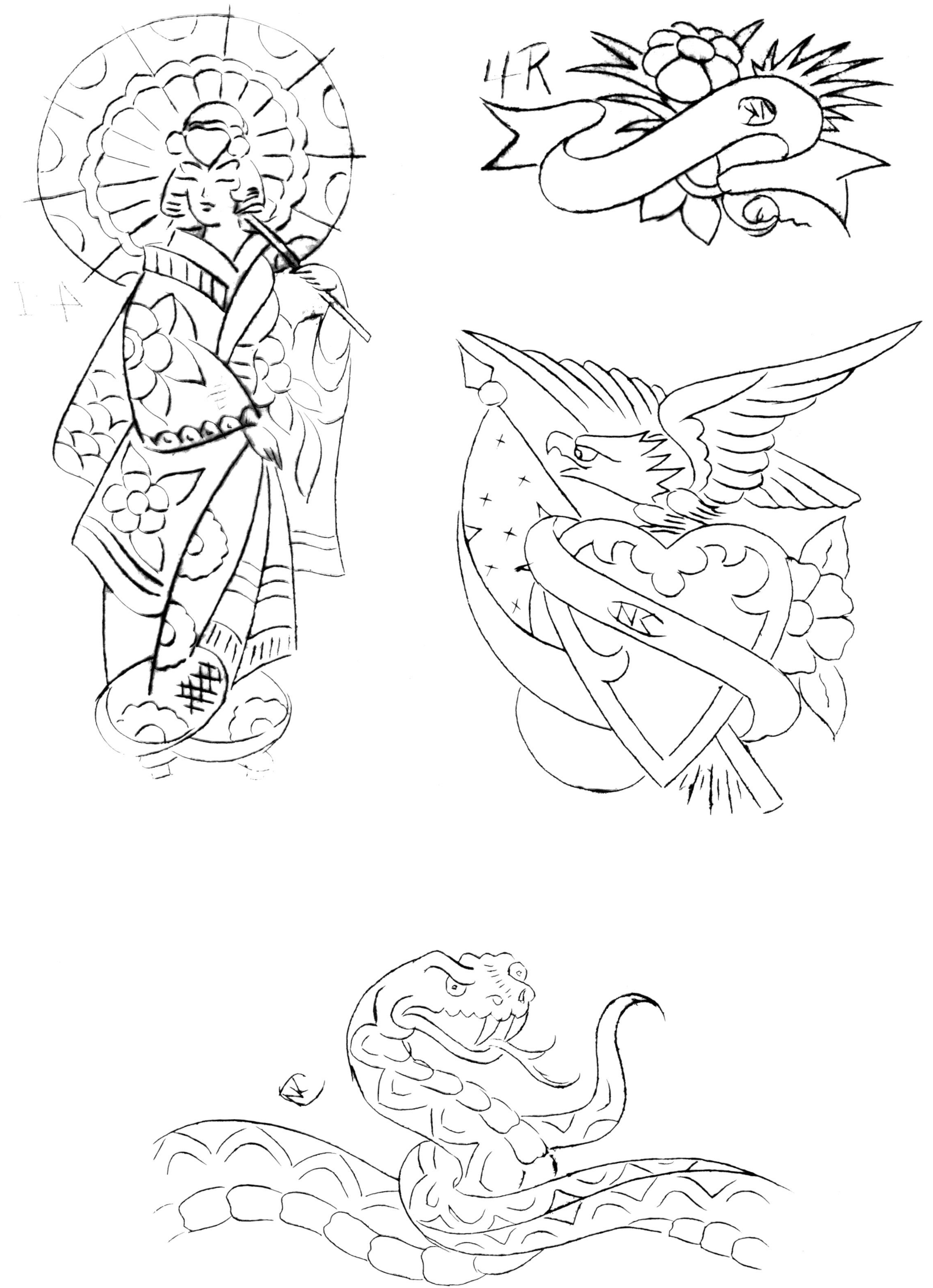
4R

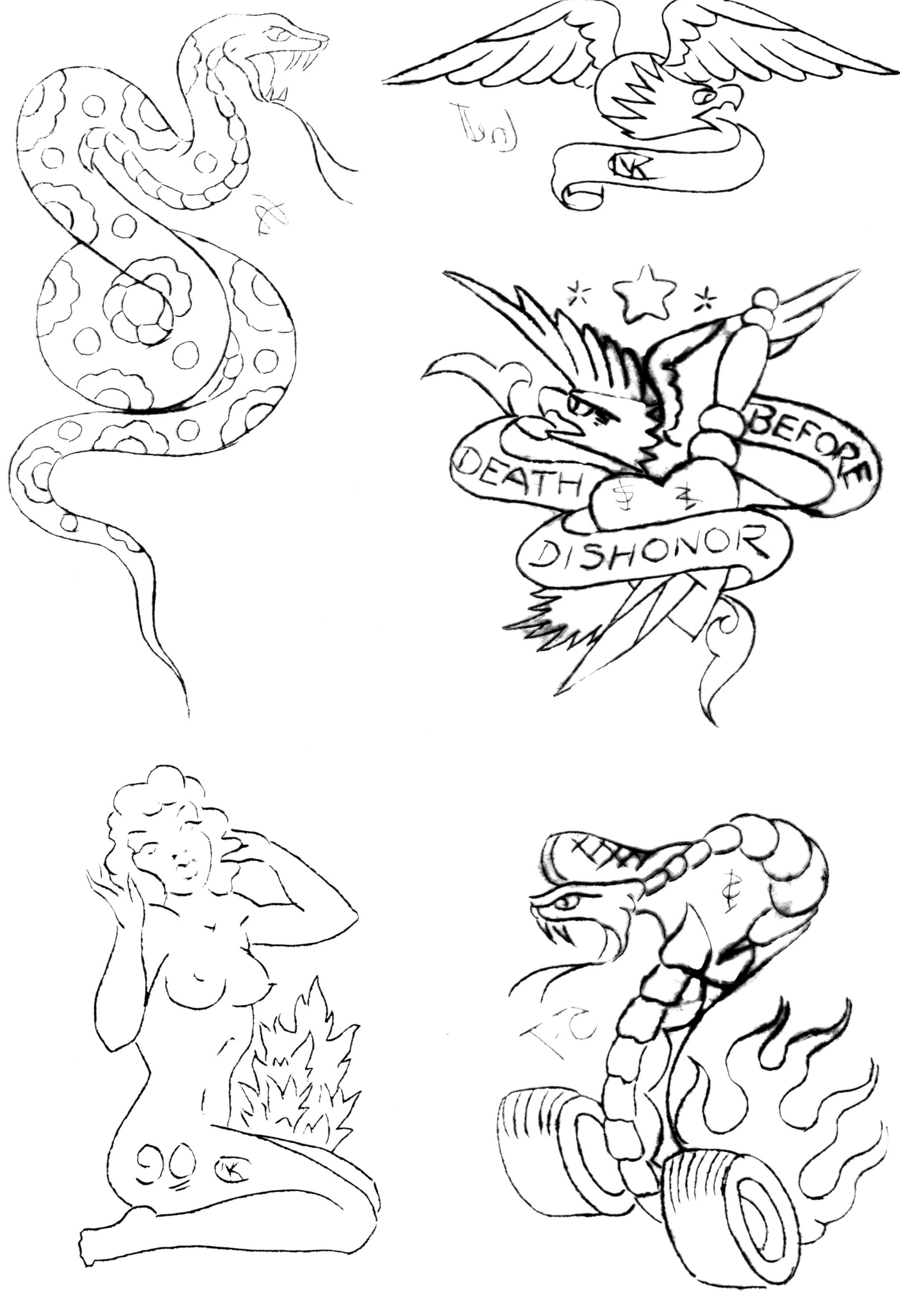
DEATH
BEFORE
DISHONOR

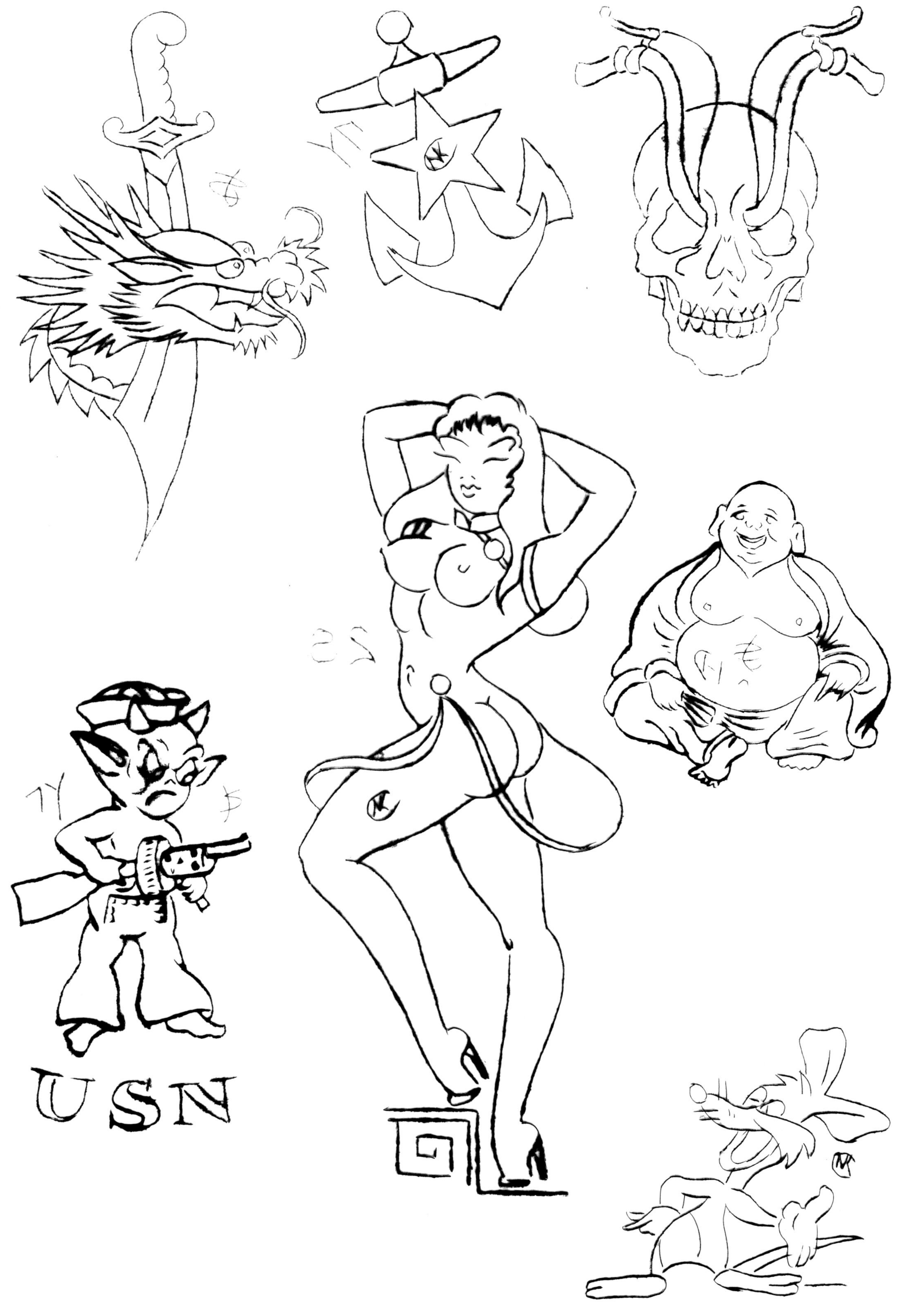
USN

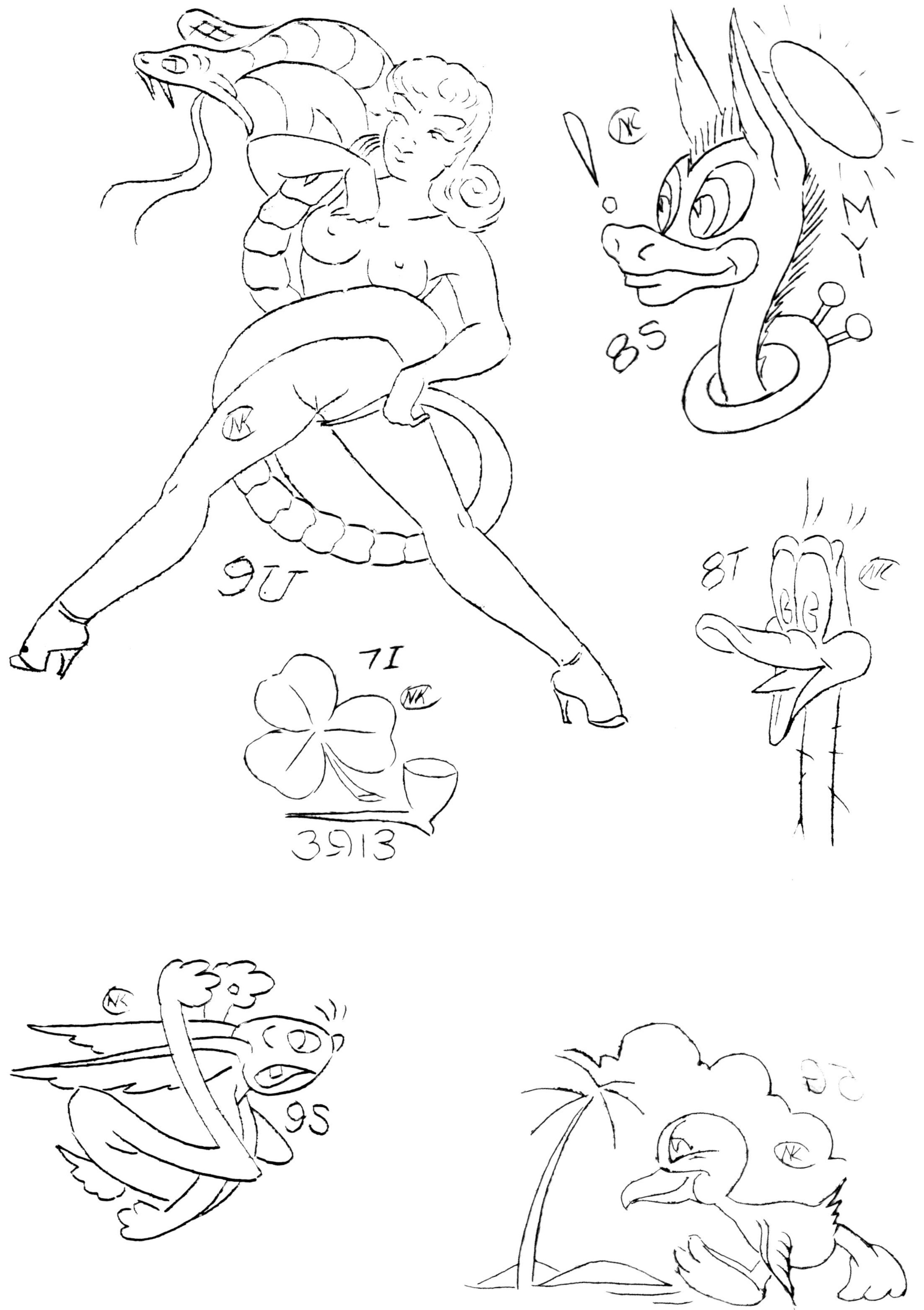
85
9U
7I
8T
3913
95

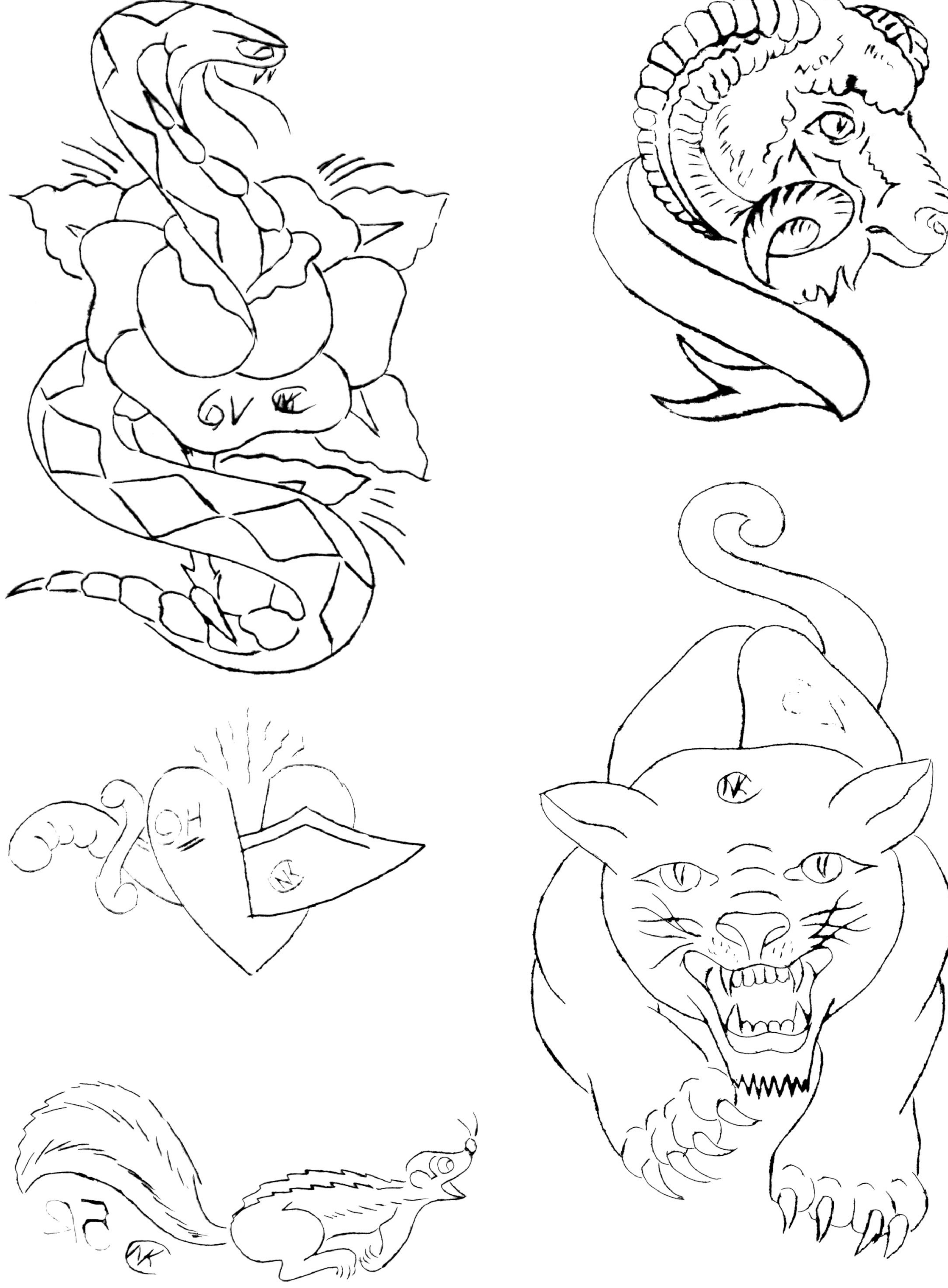

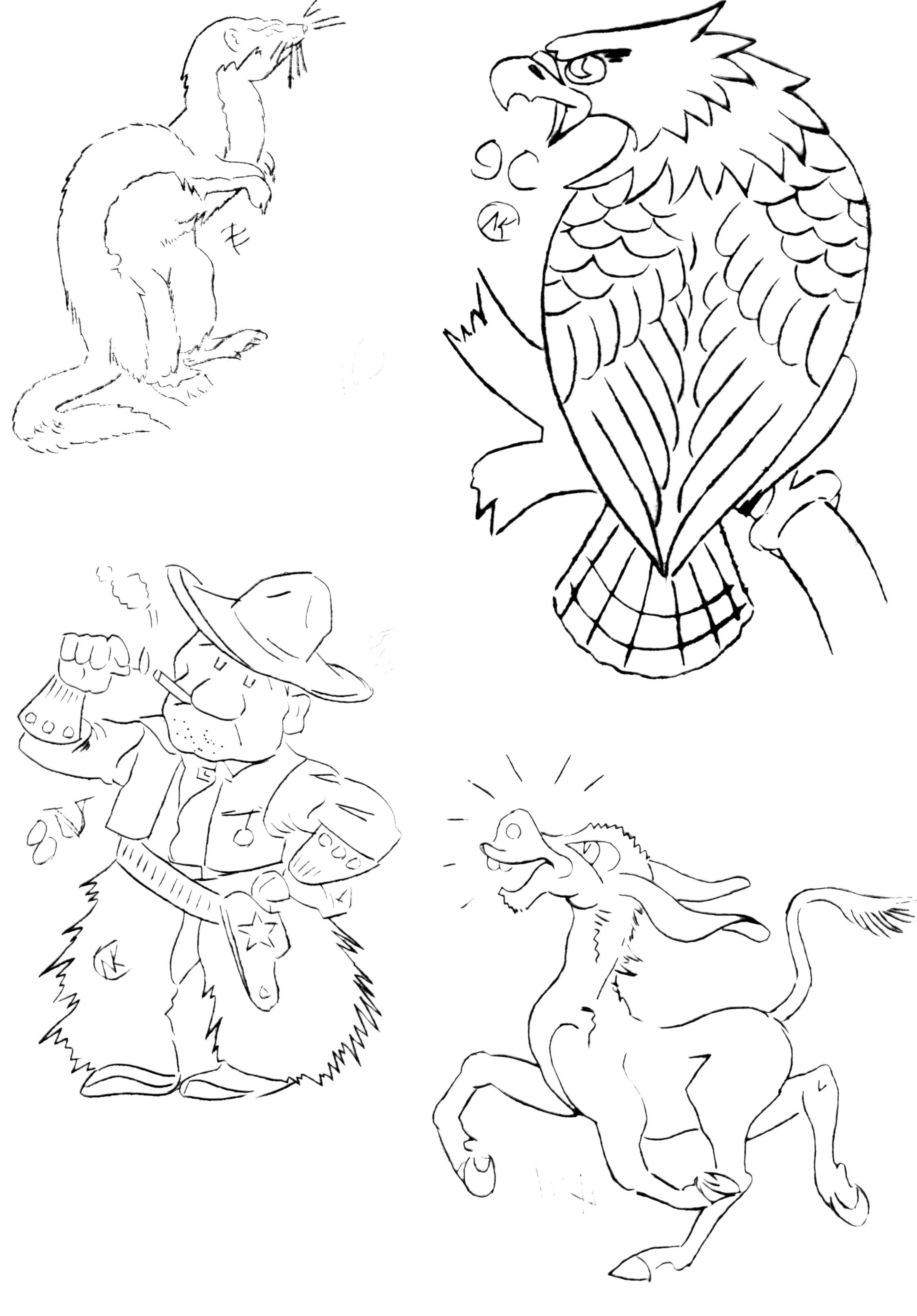

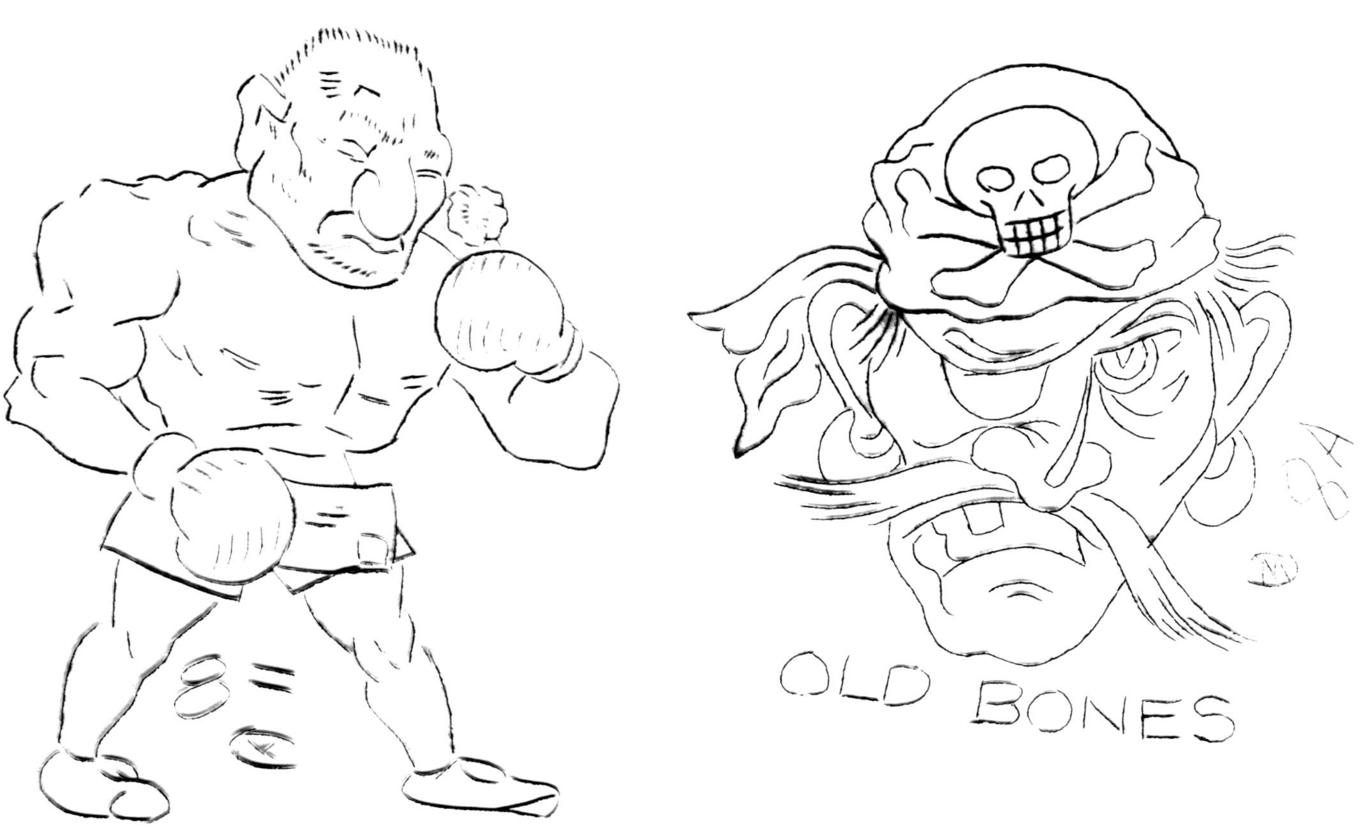
OLD BONES

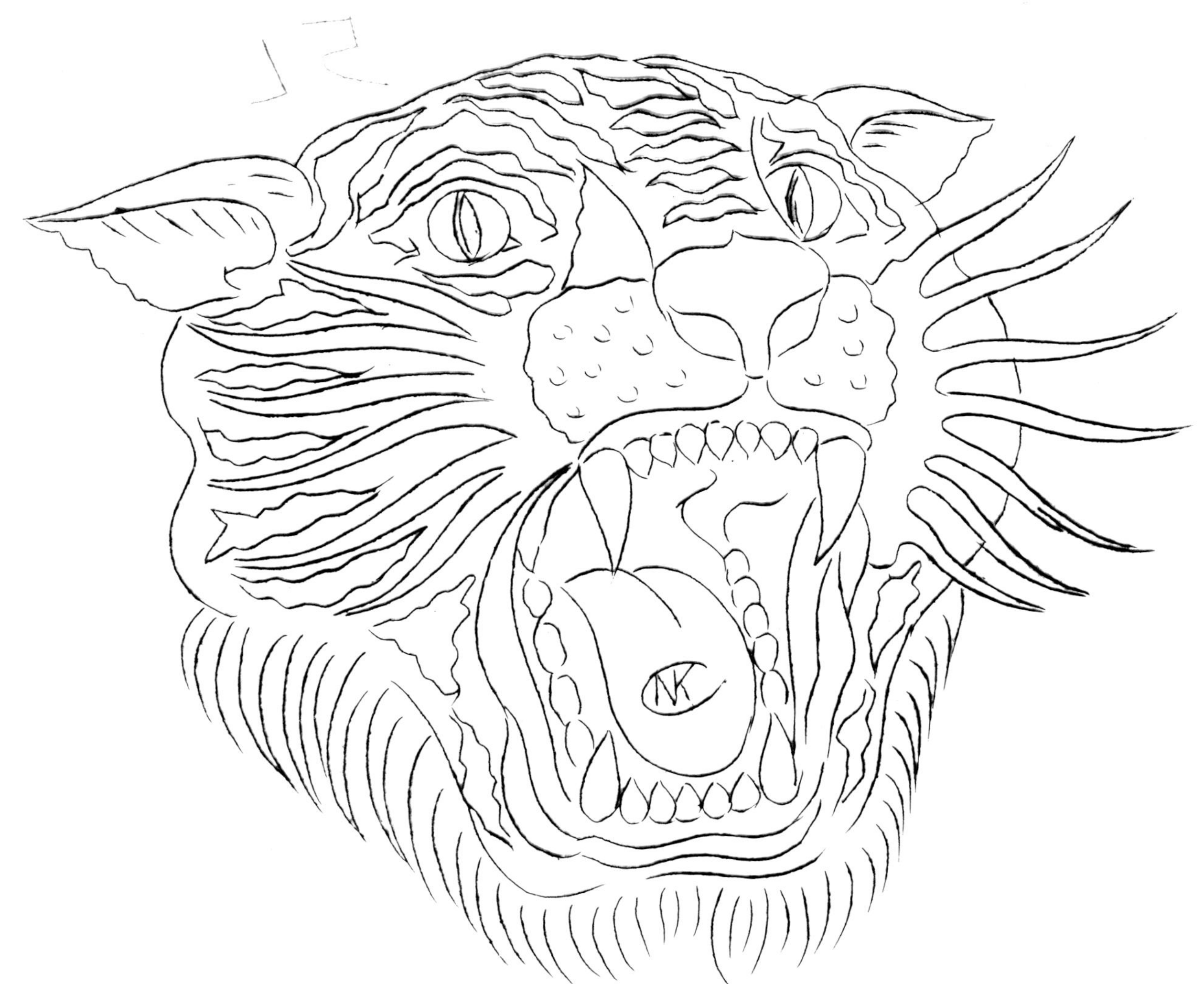

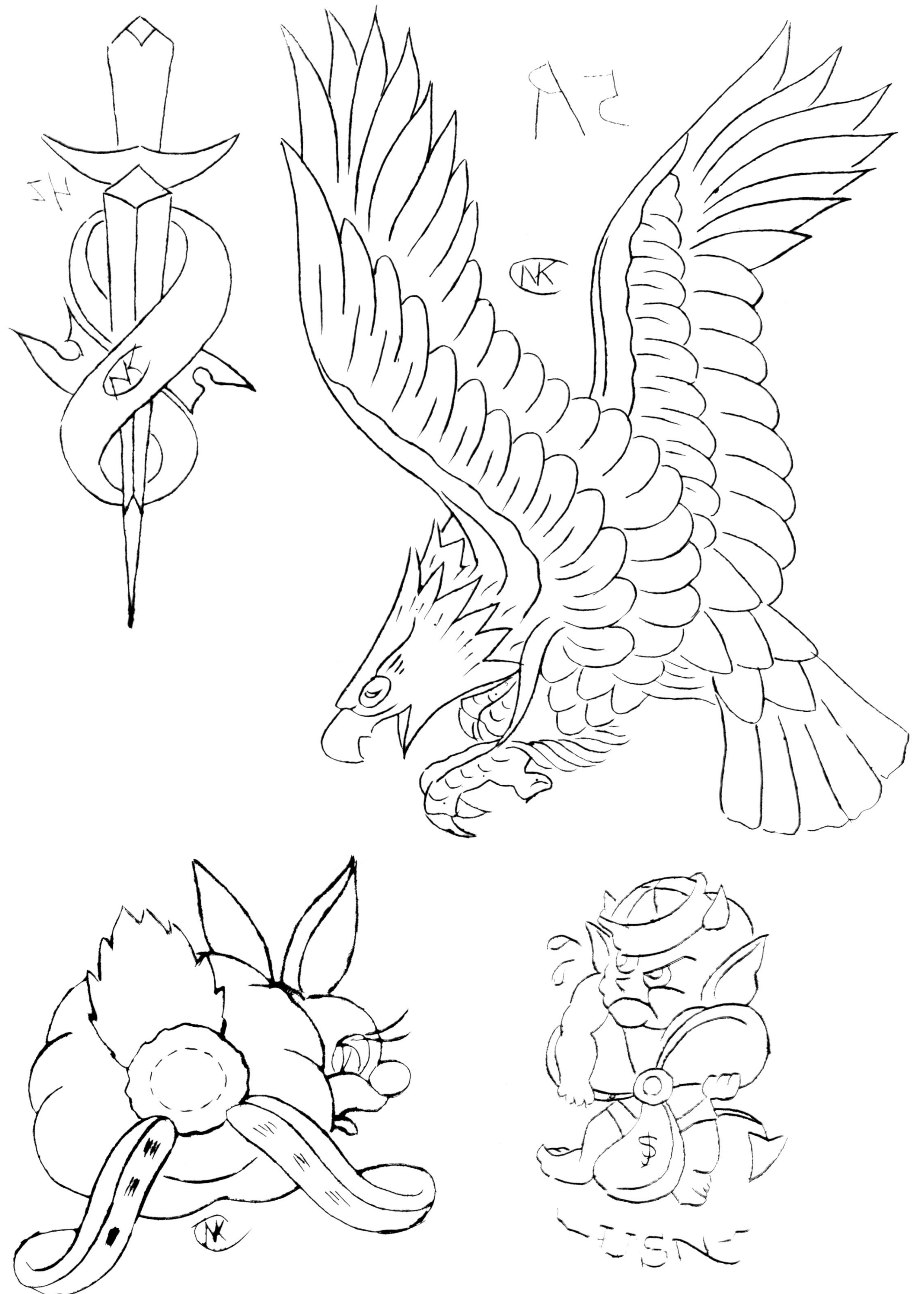

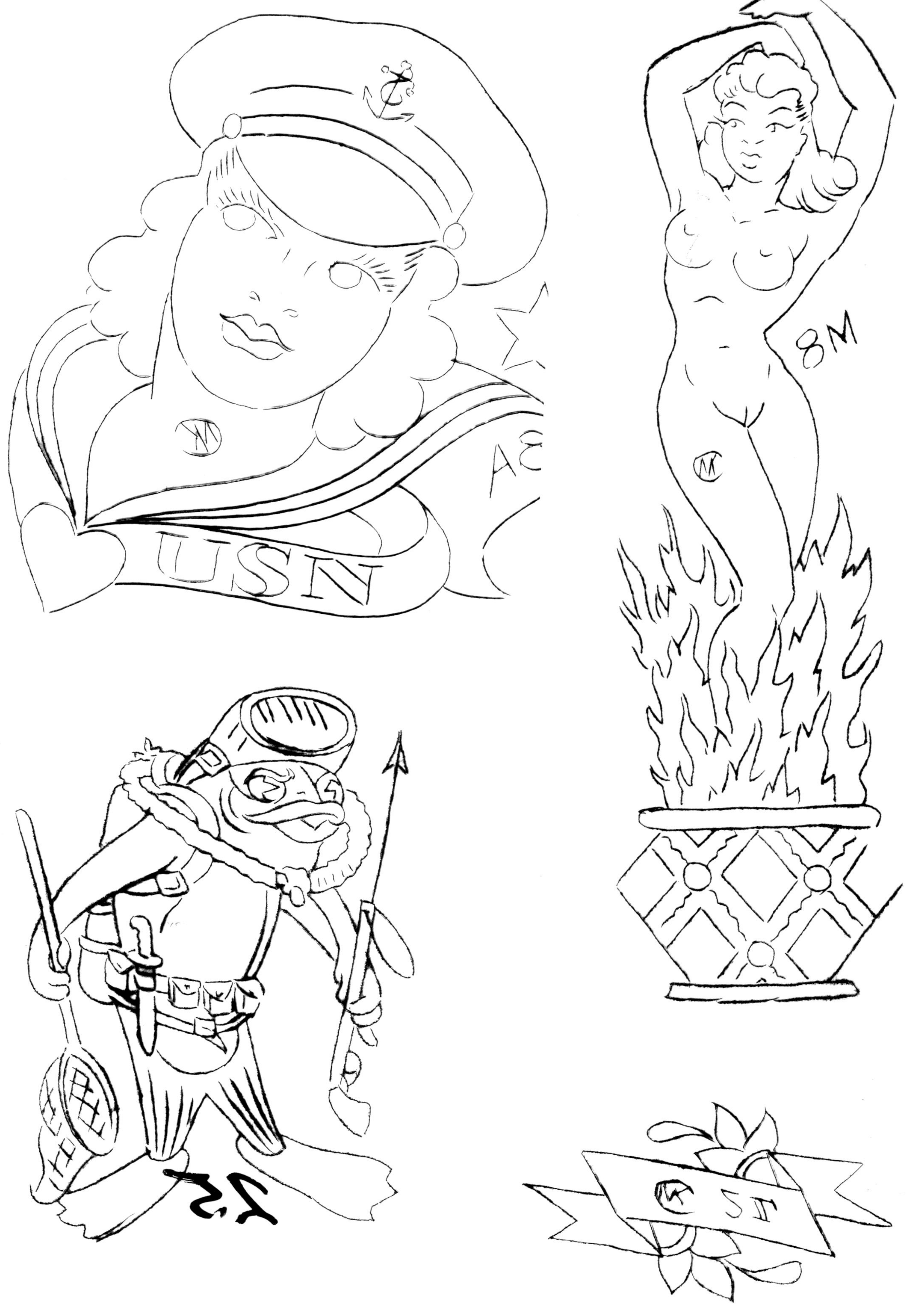
USN
8M

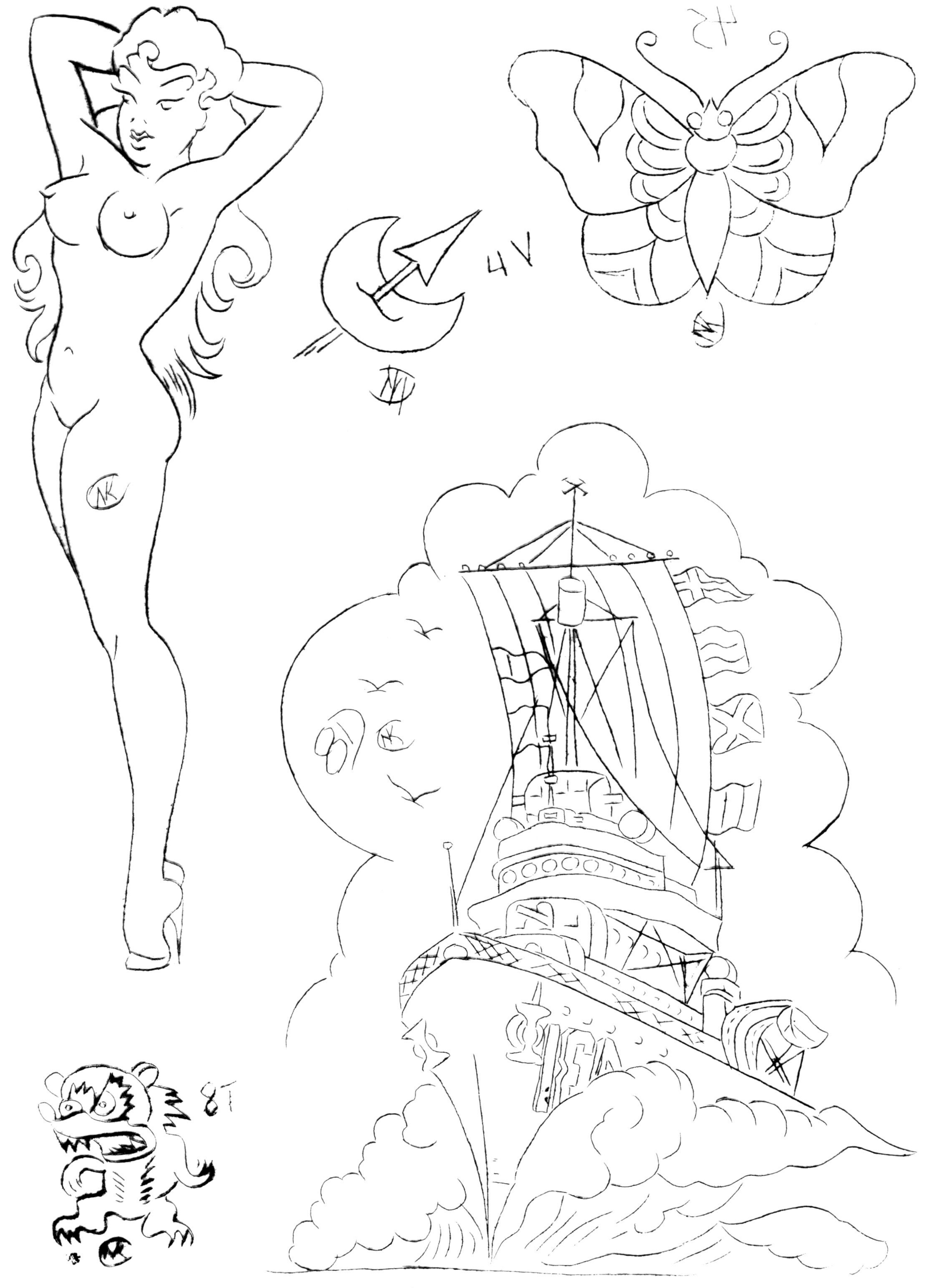

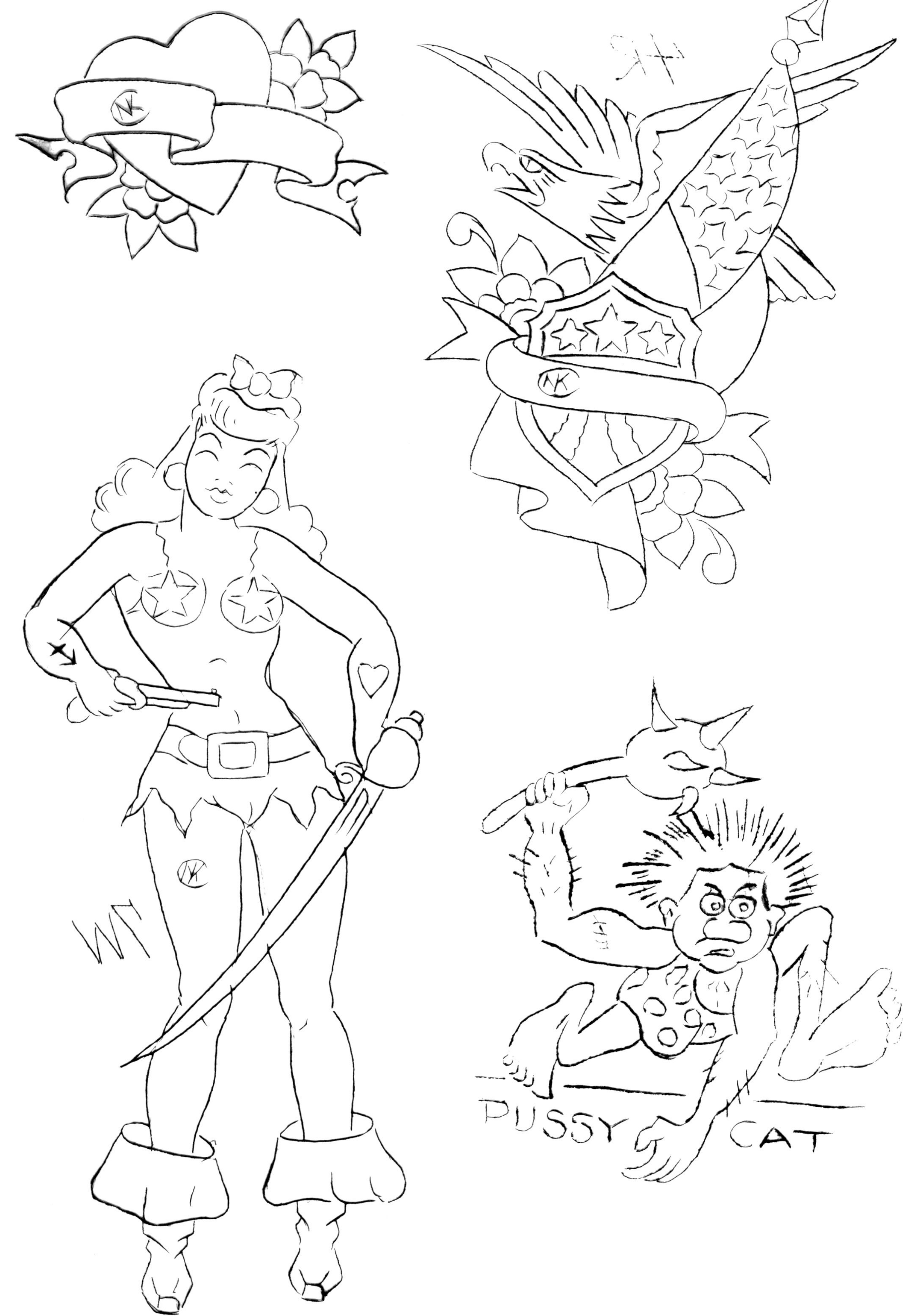
PUSSY CAT

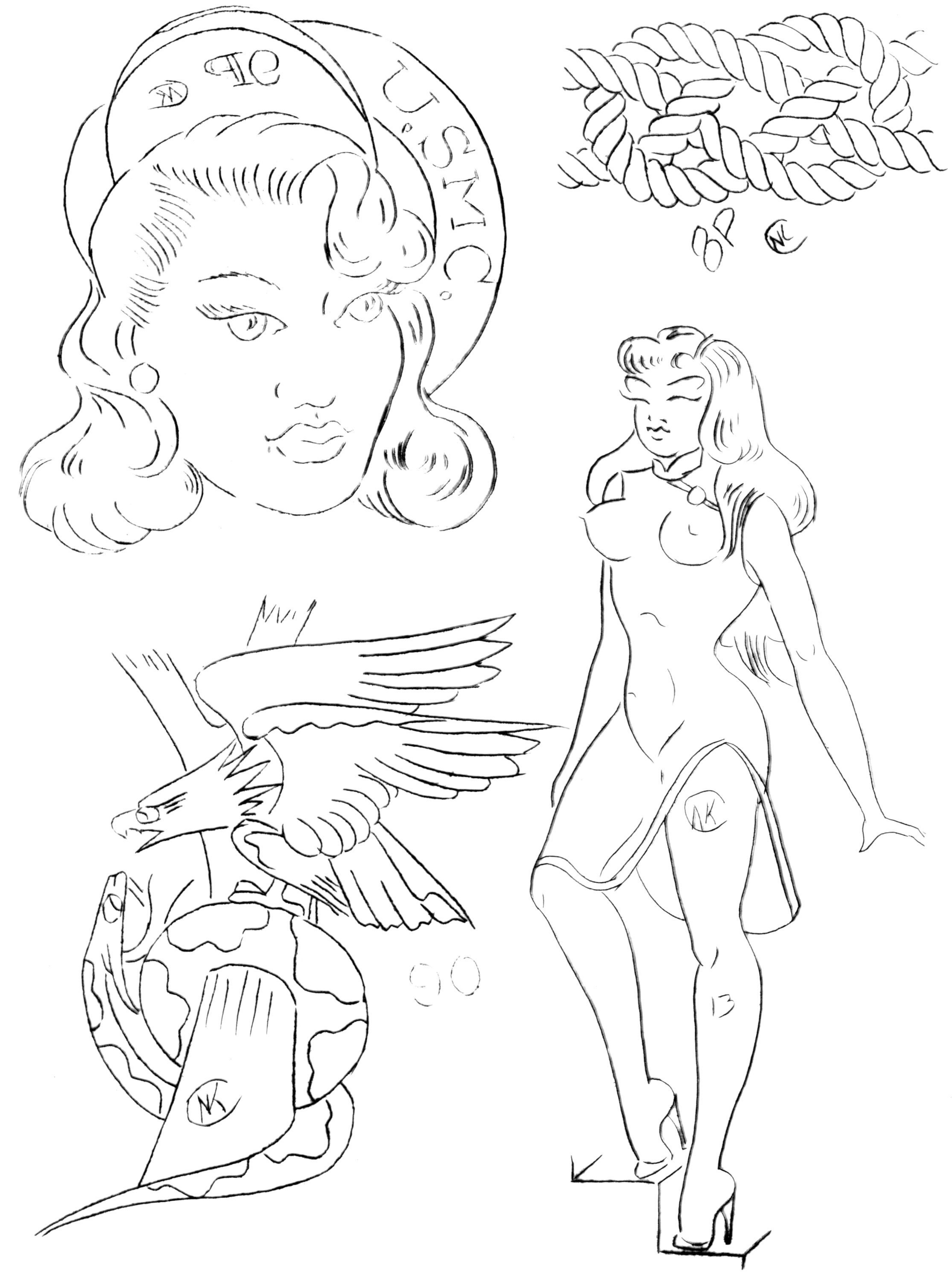
U.S.M.C.

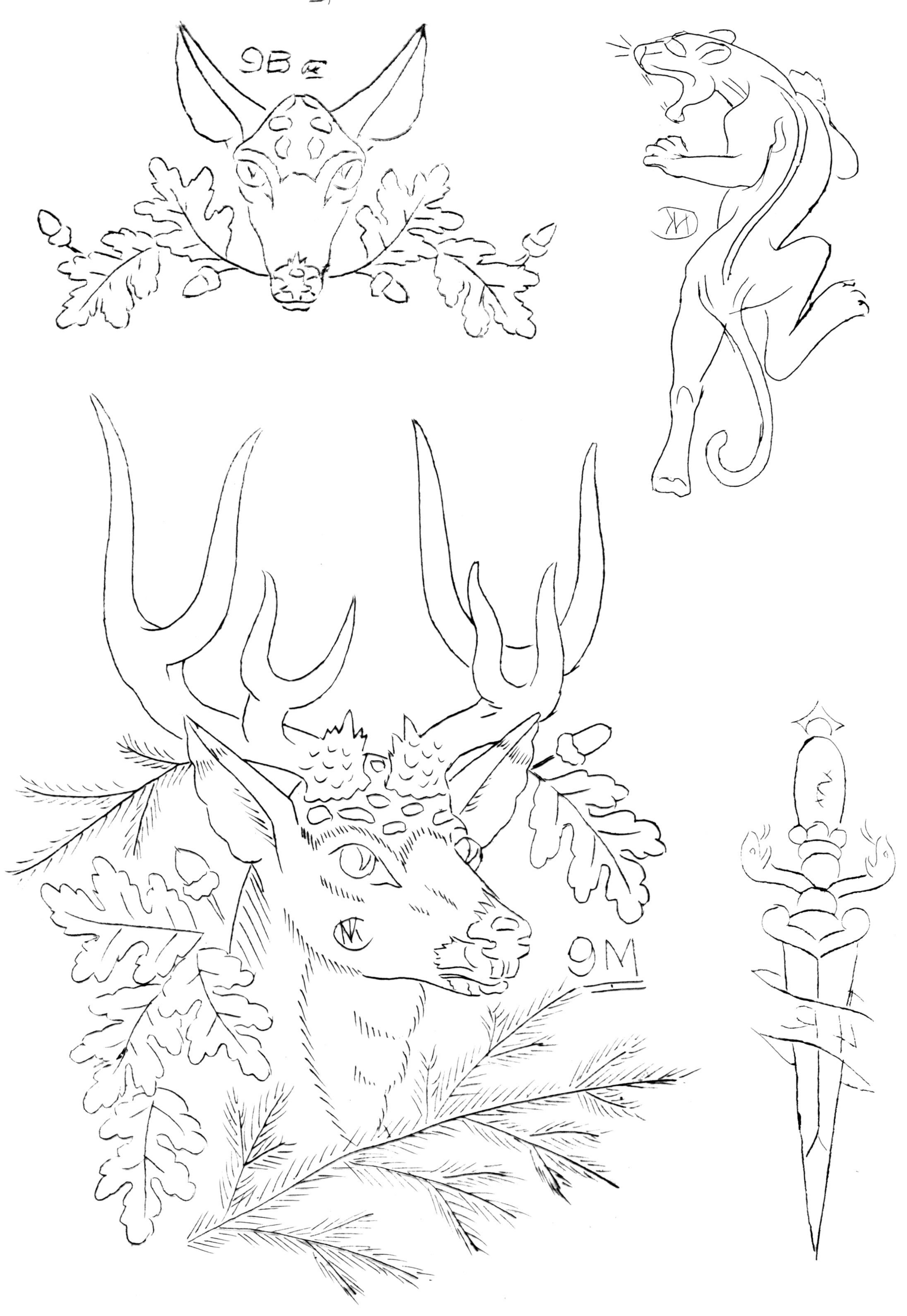
9B
9M

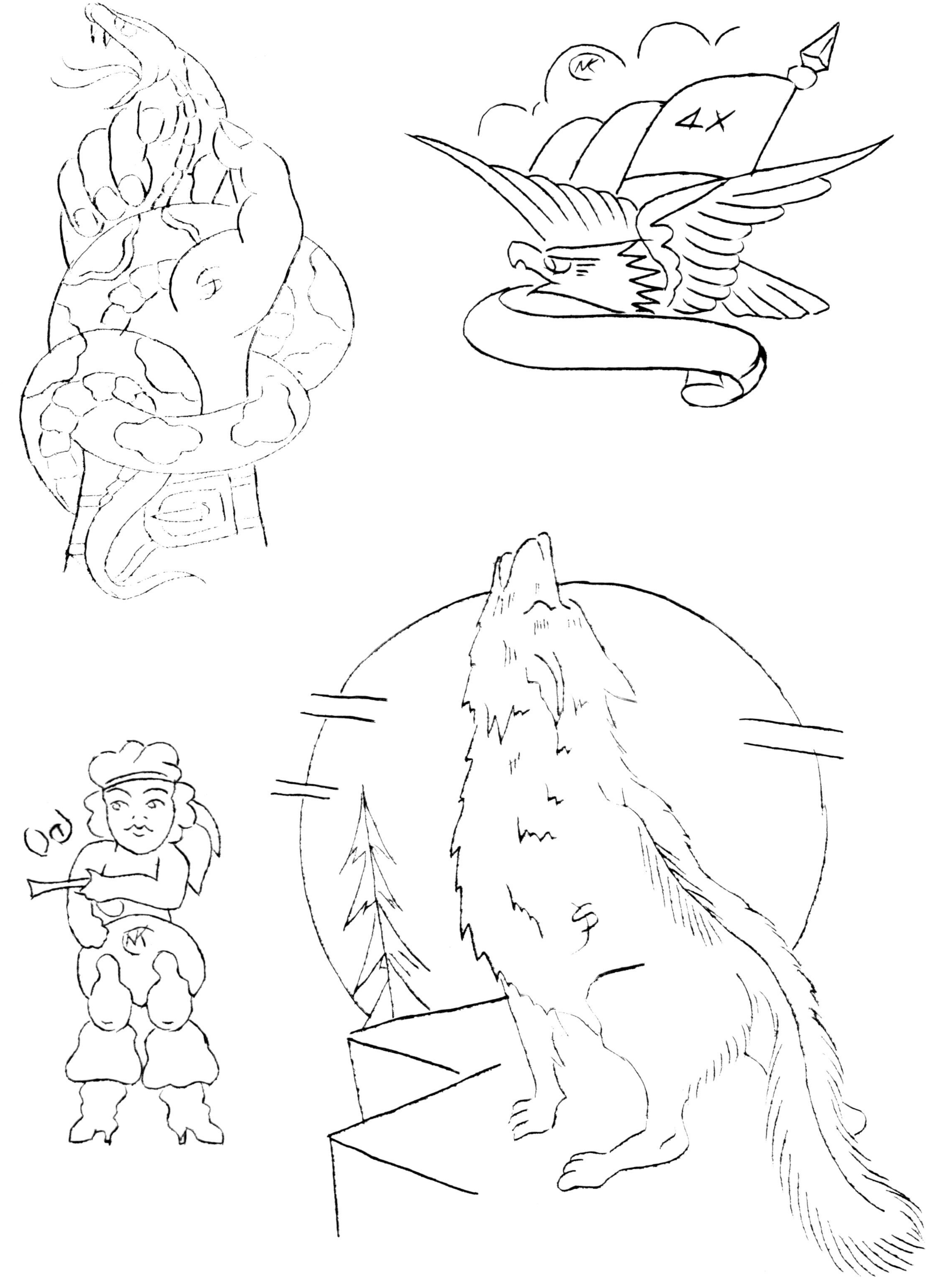
4X

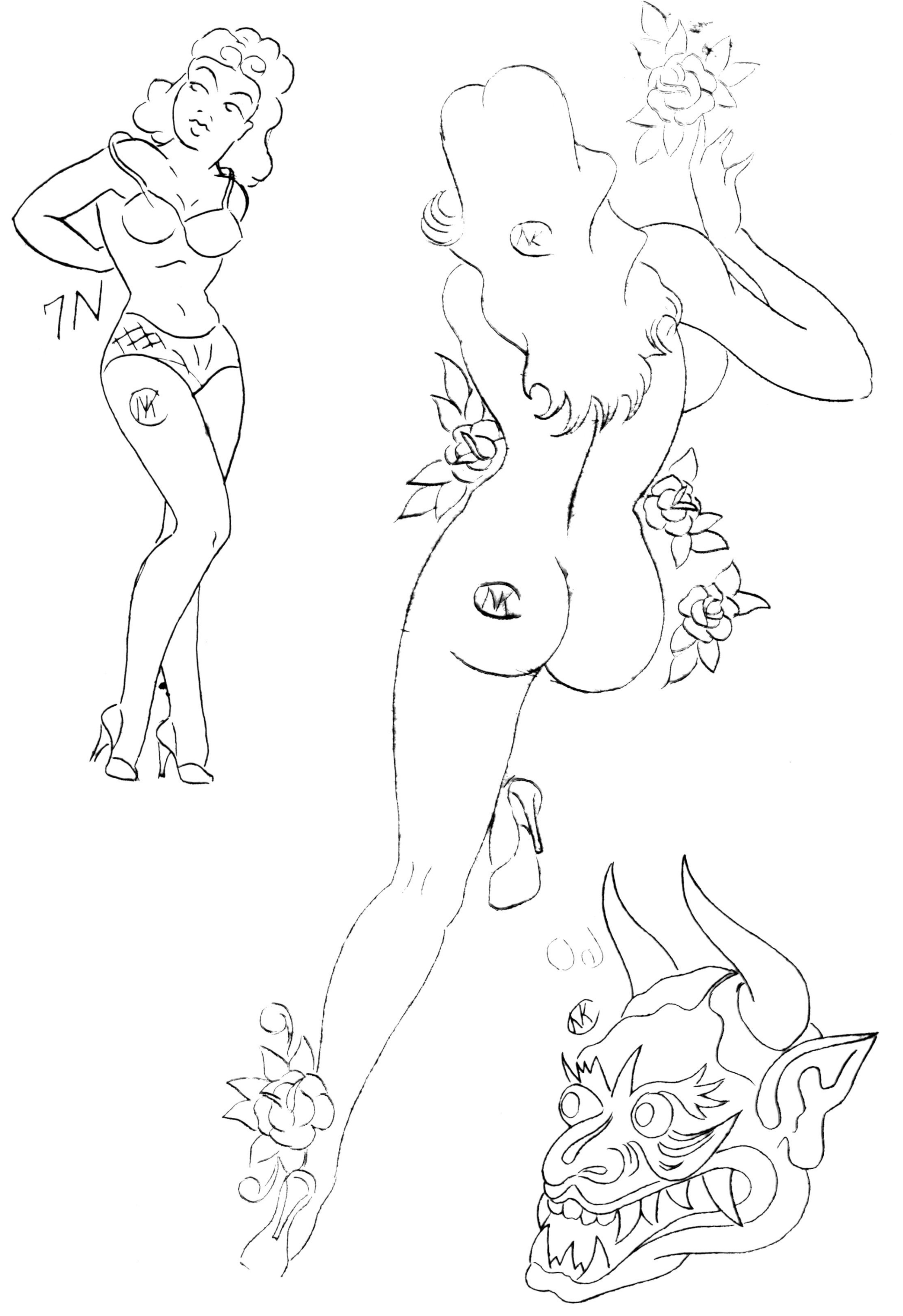
7N

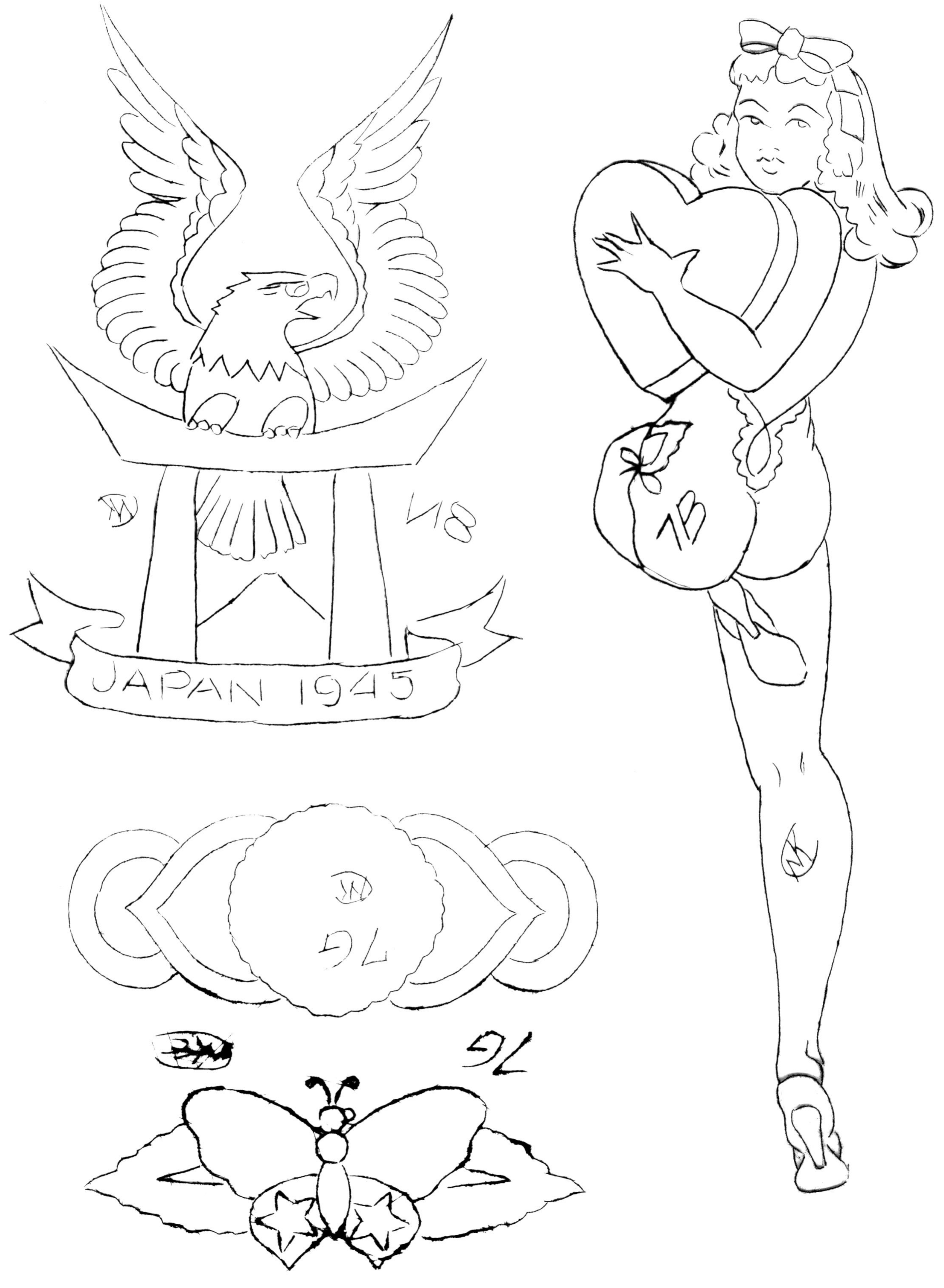
JAPAN 1945

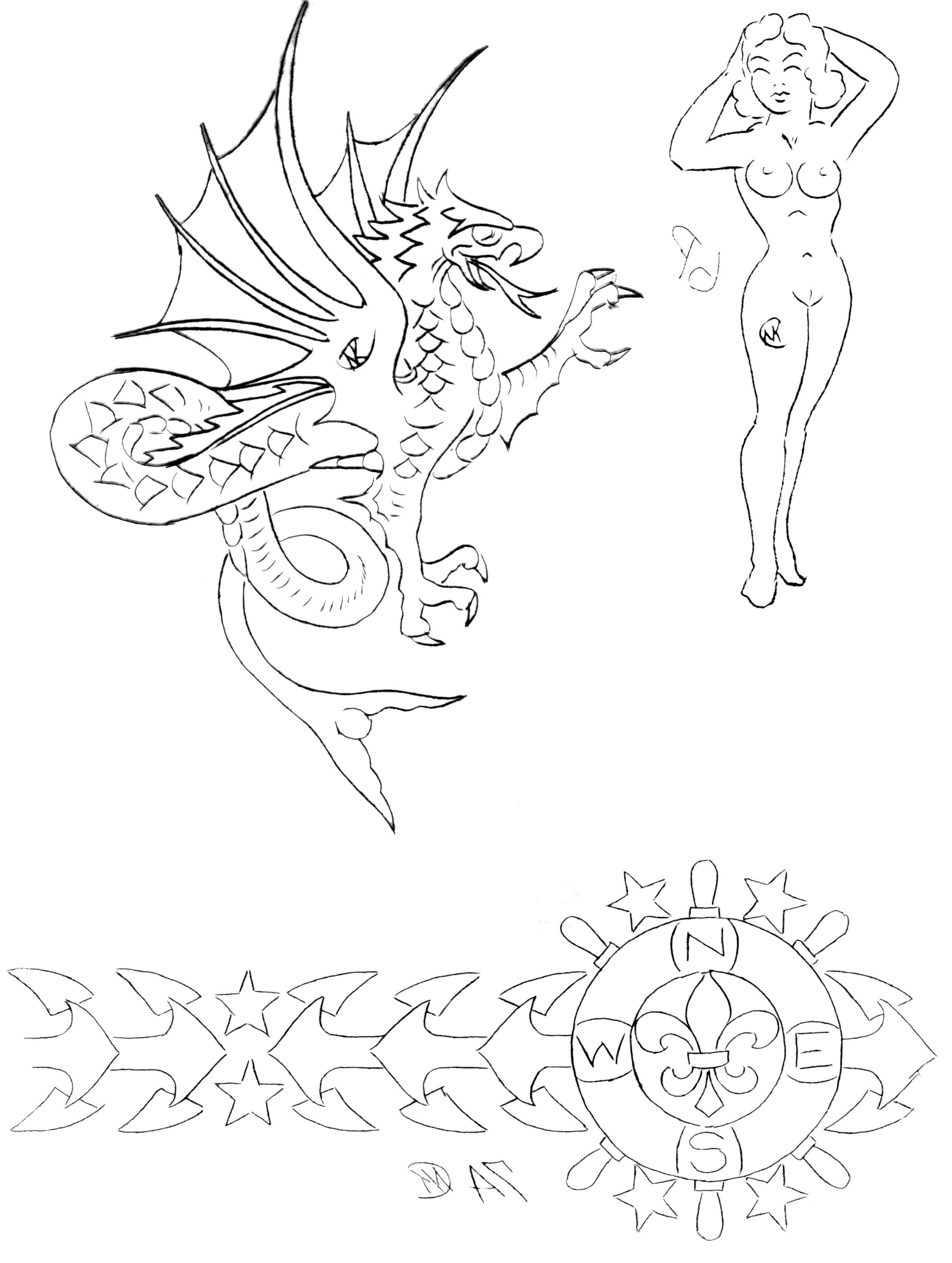
N
W
E
S

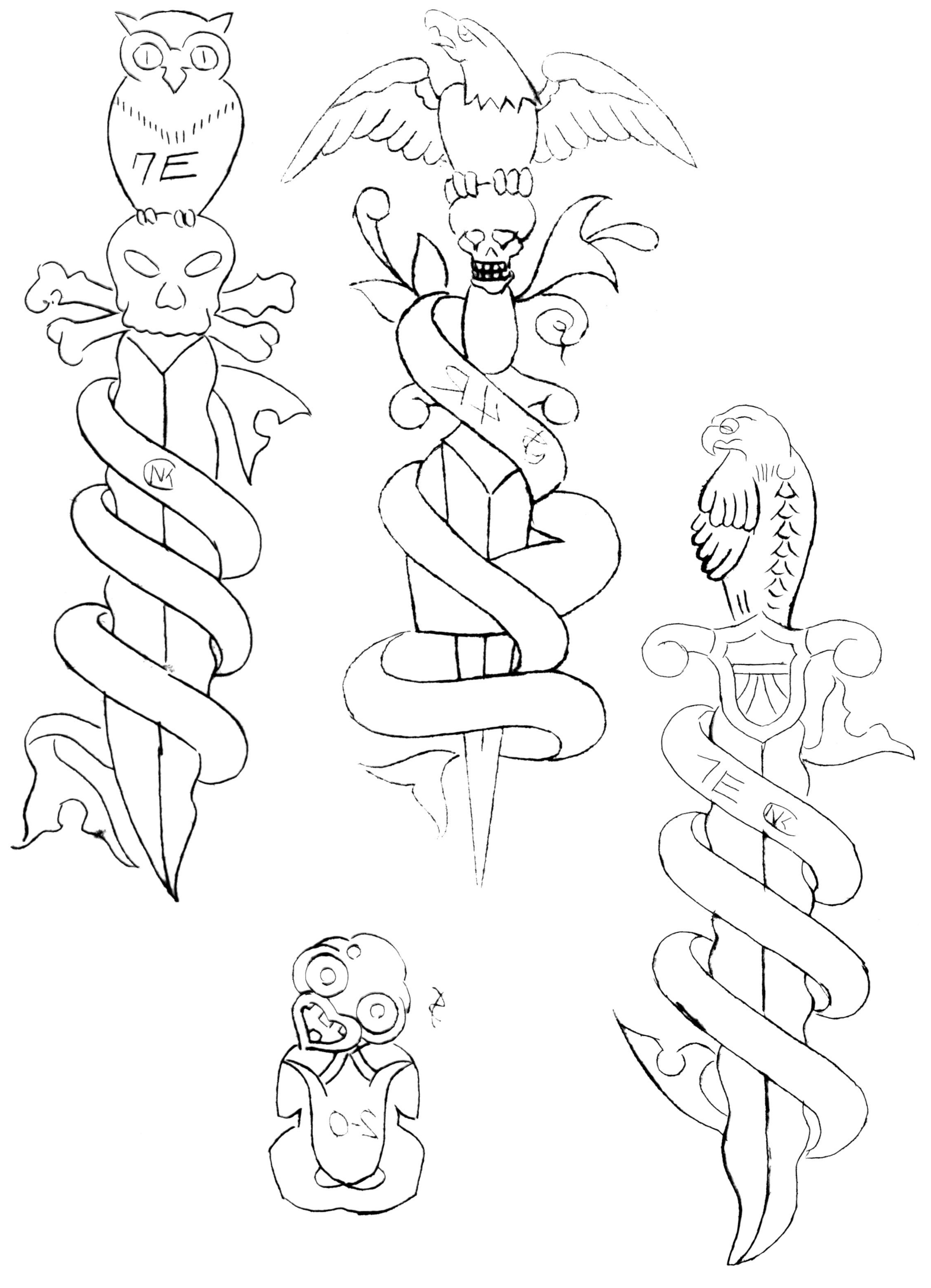
7E
7E

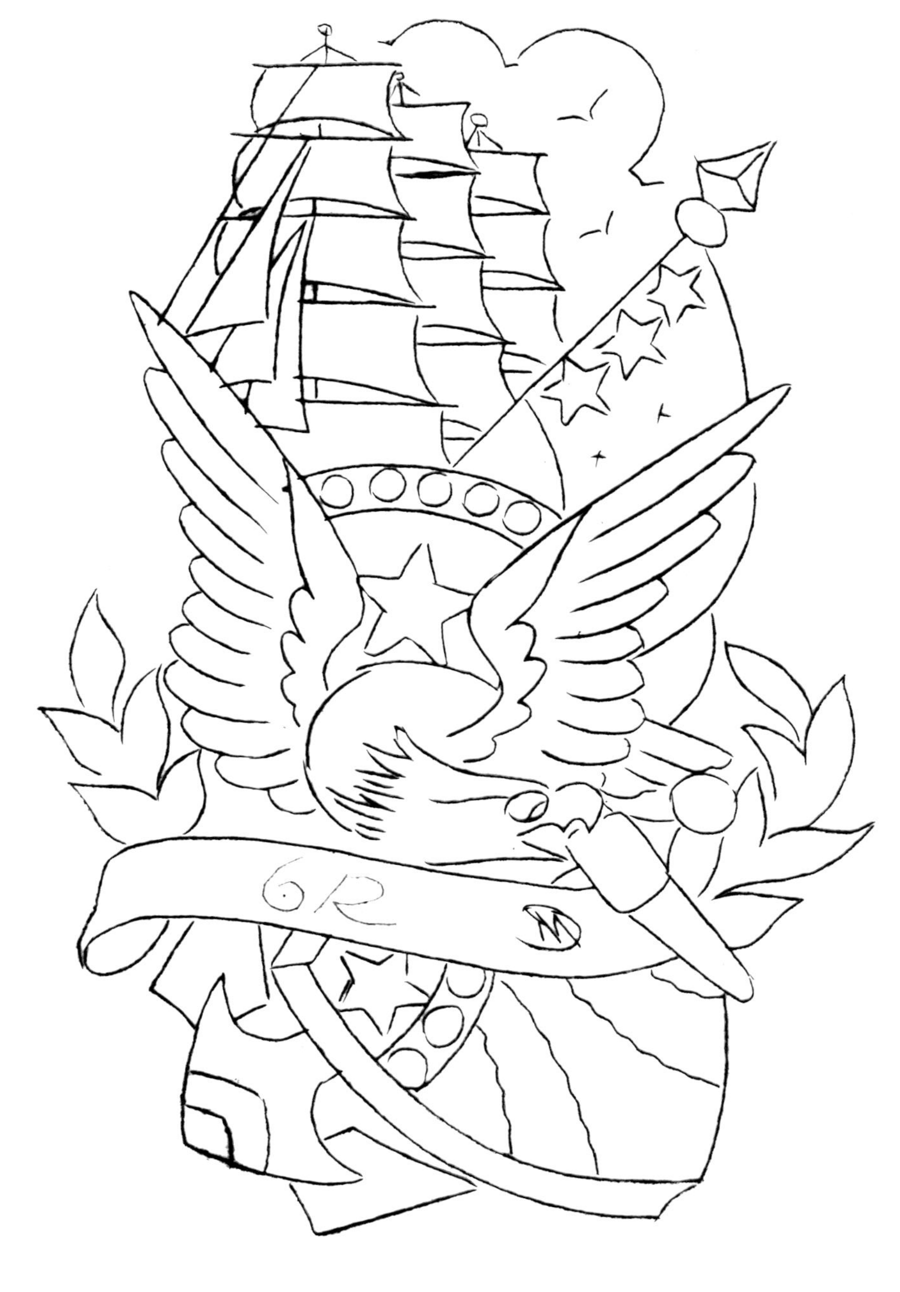

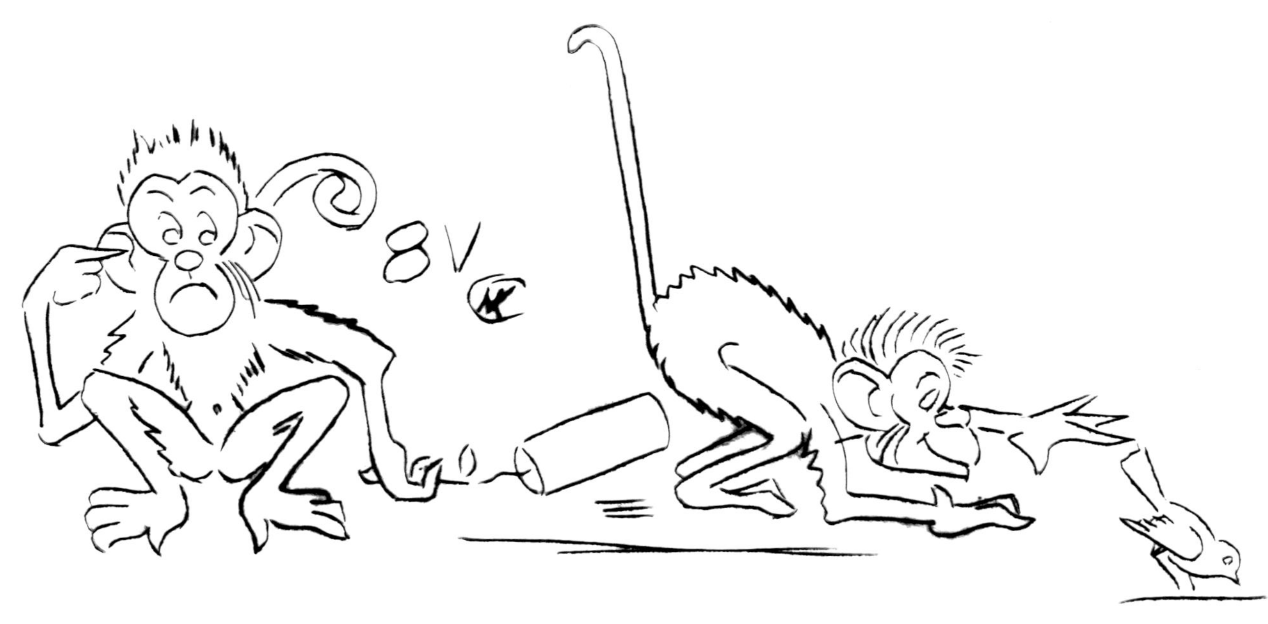

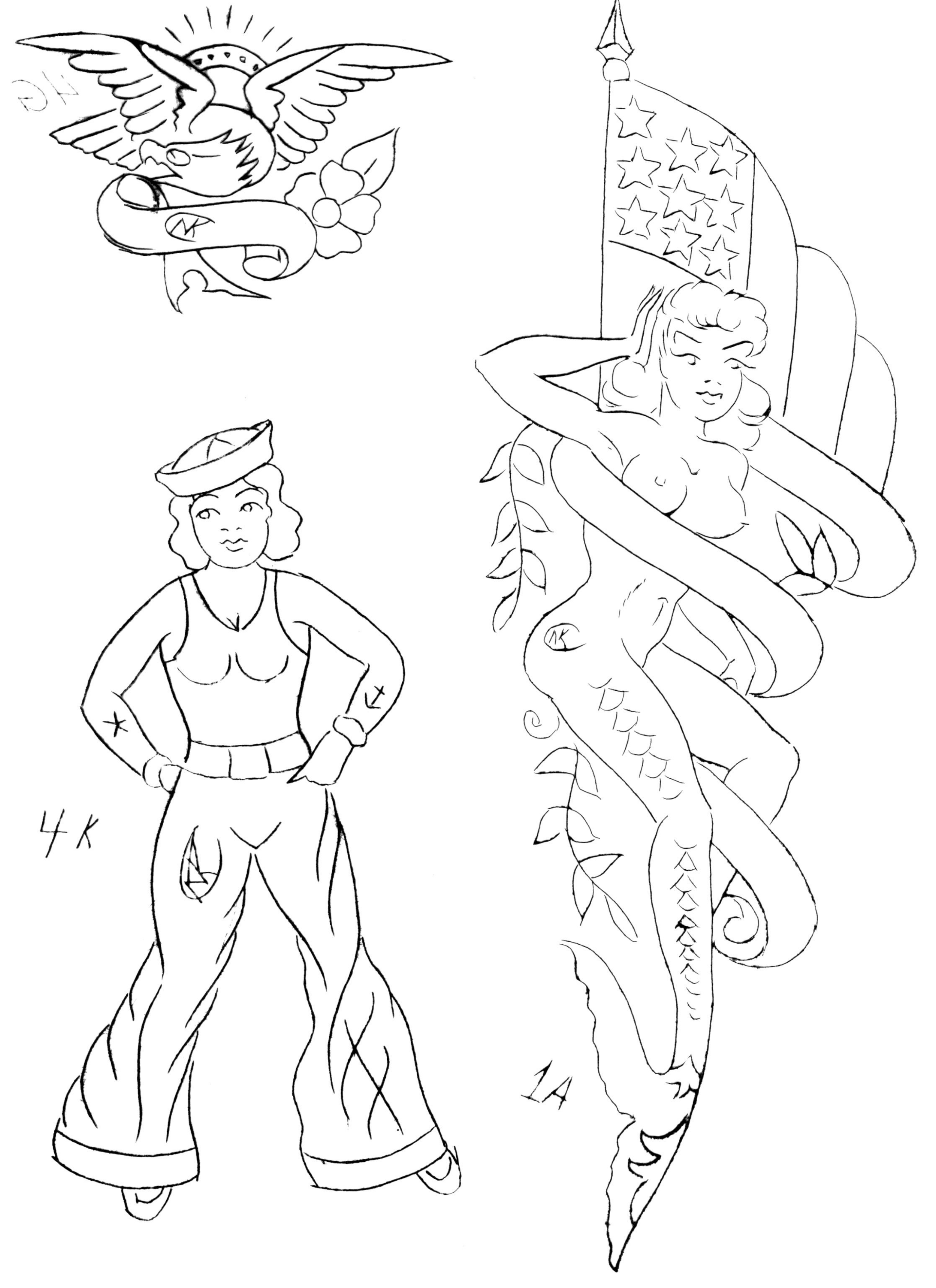
4K
1A

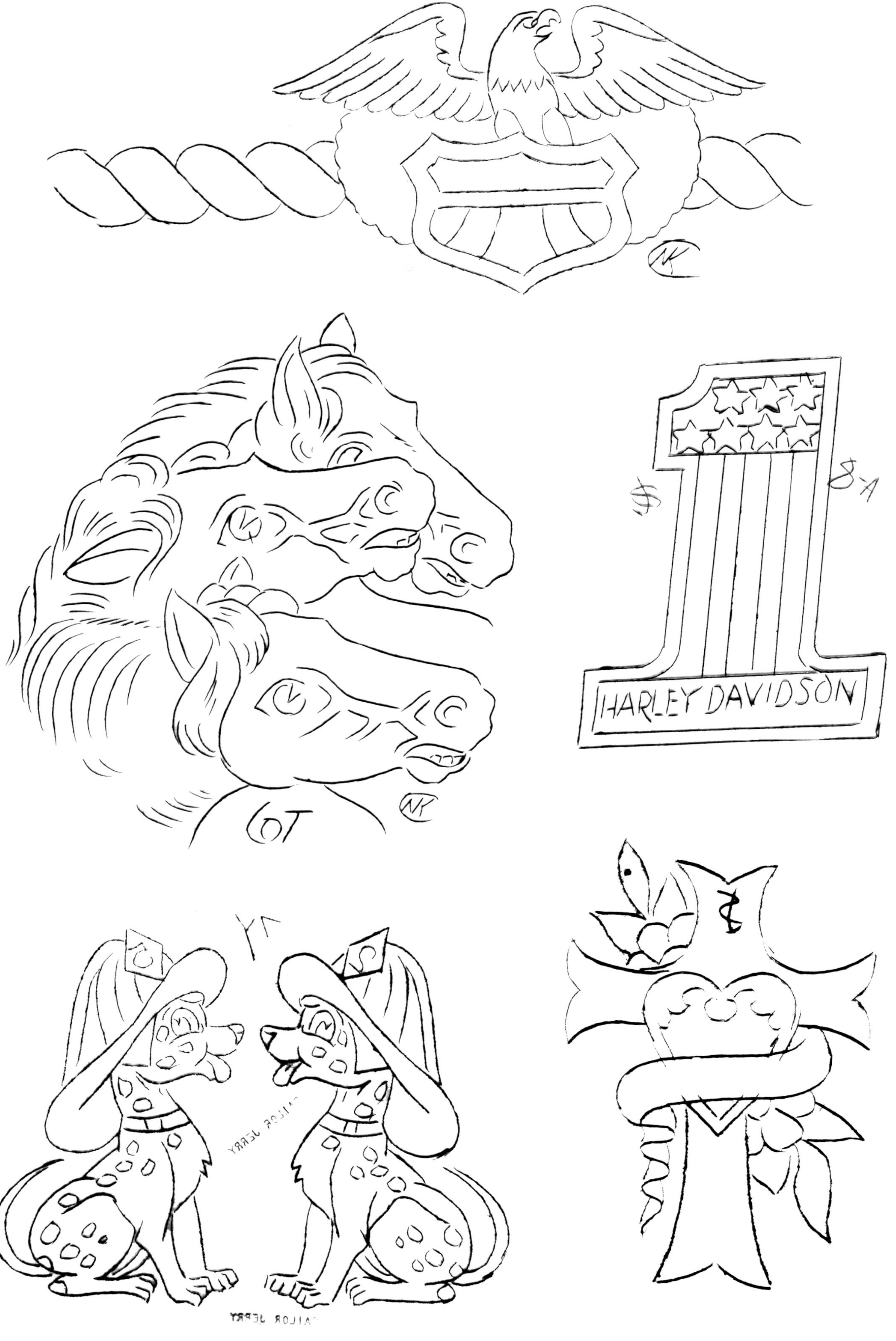
HARLEY DAVIDSON

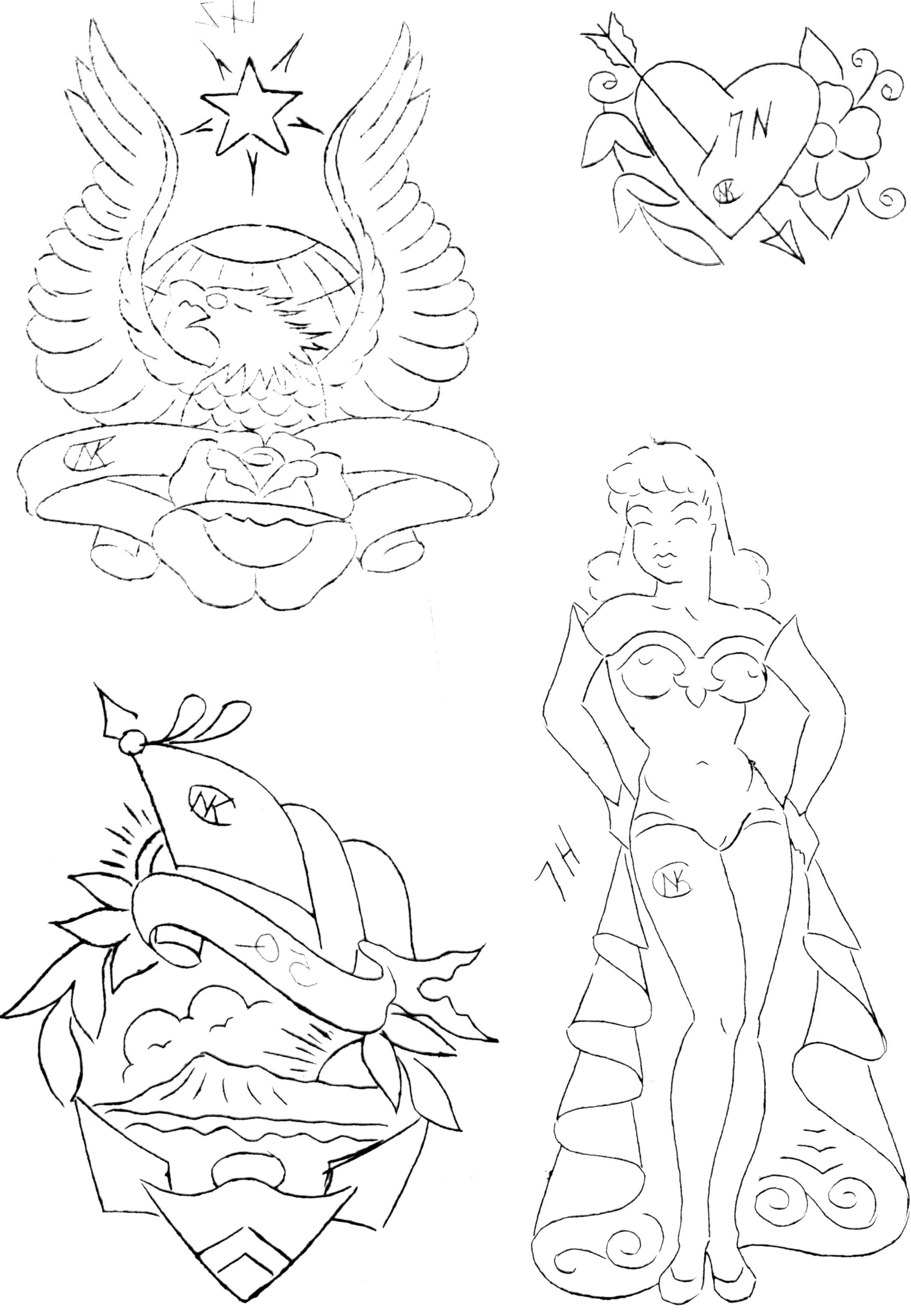

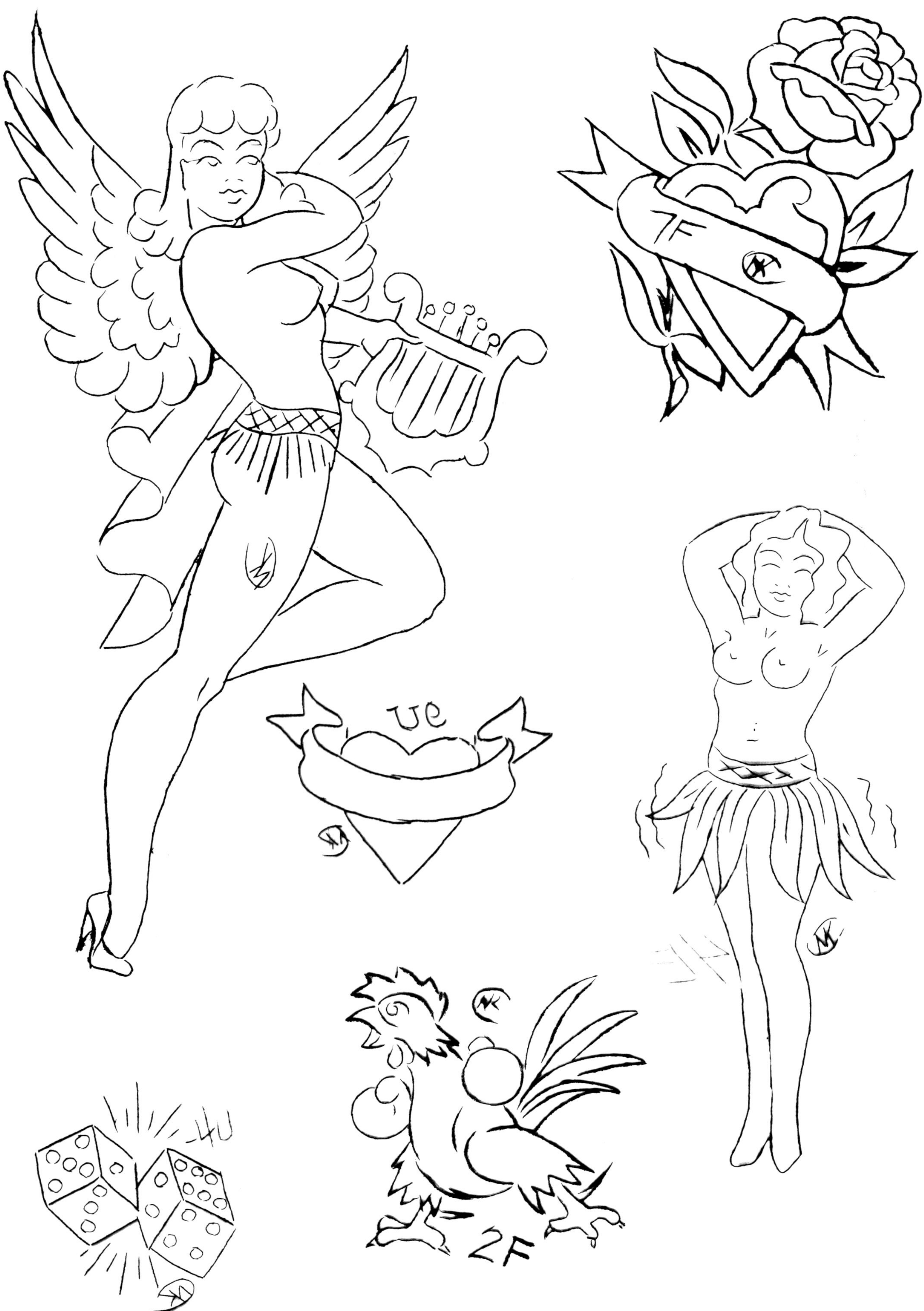
7F
2F

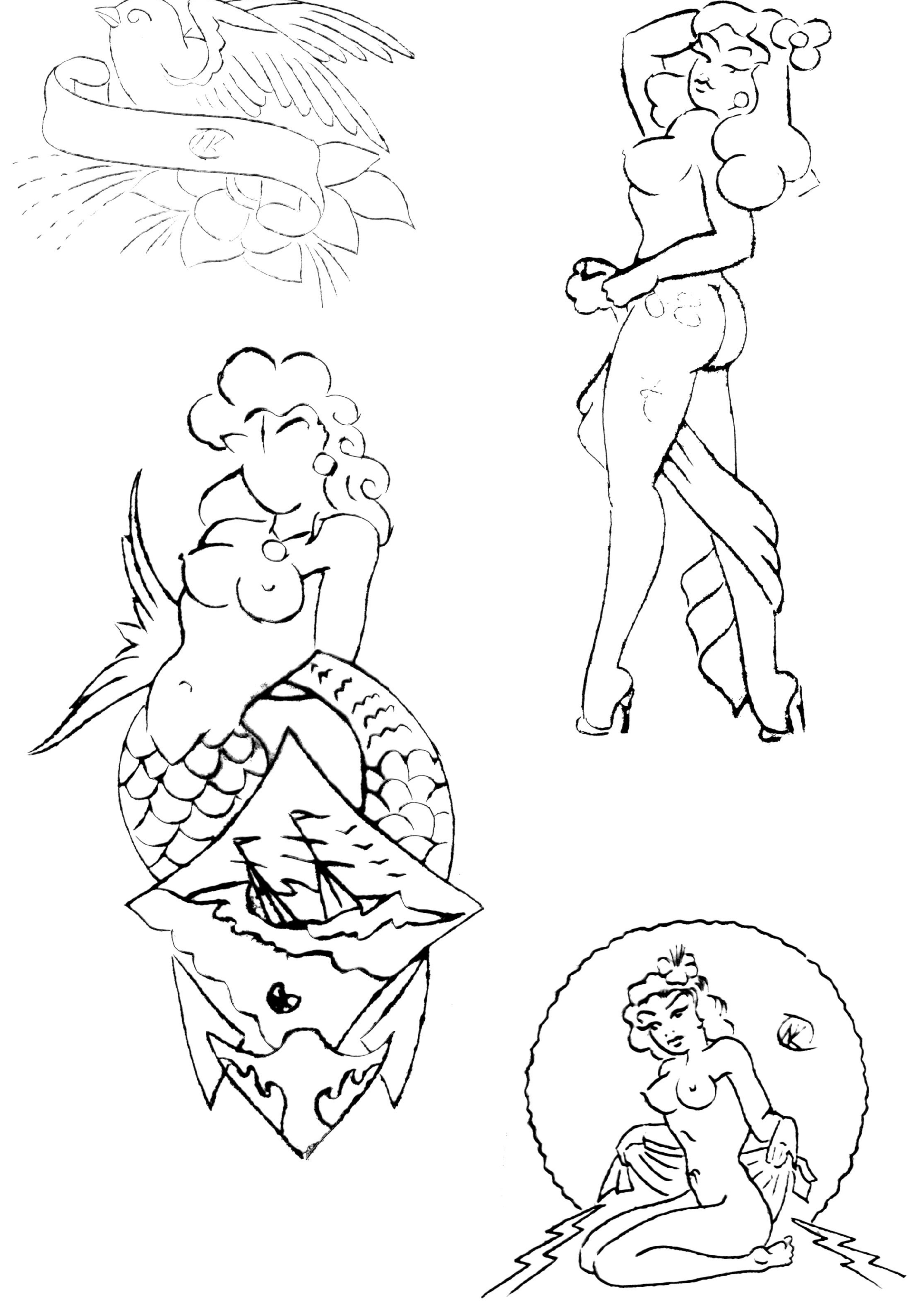

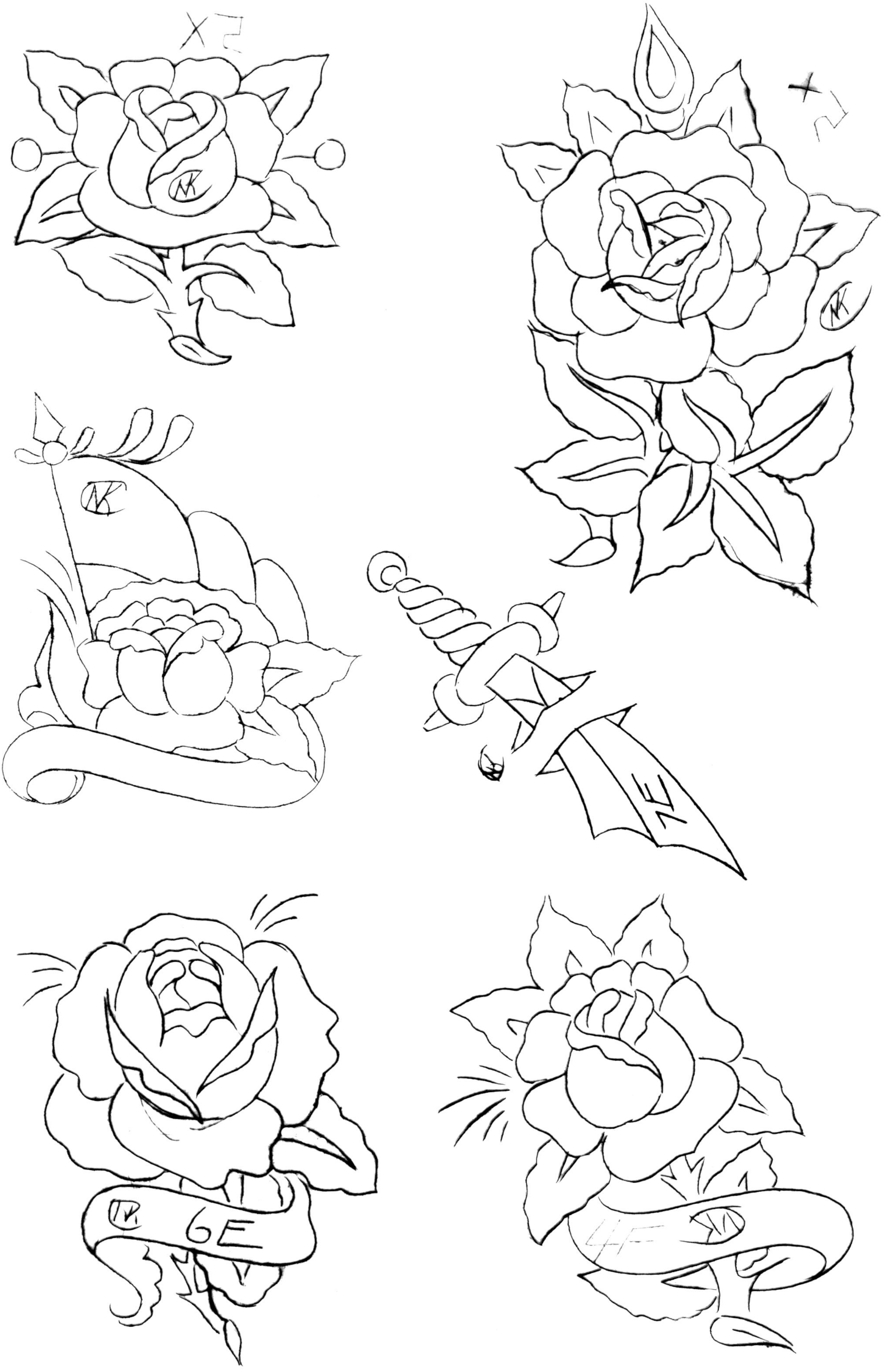

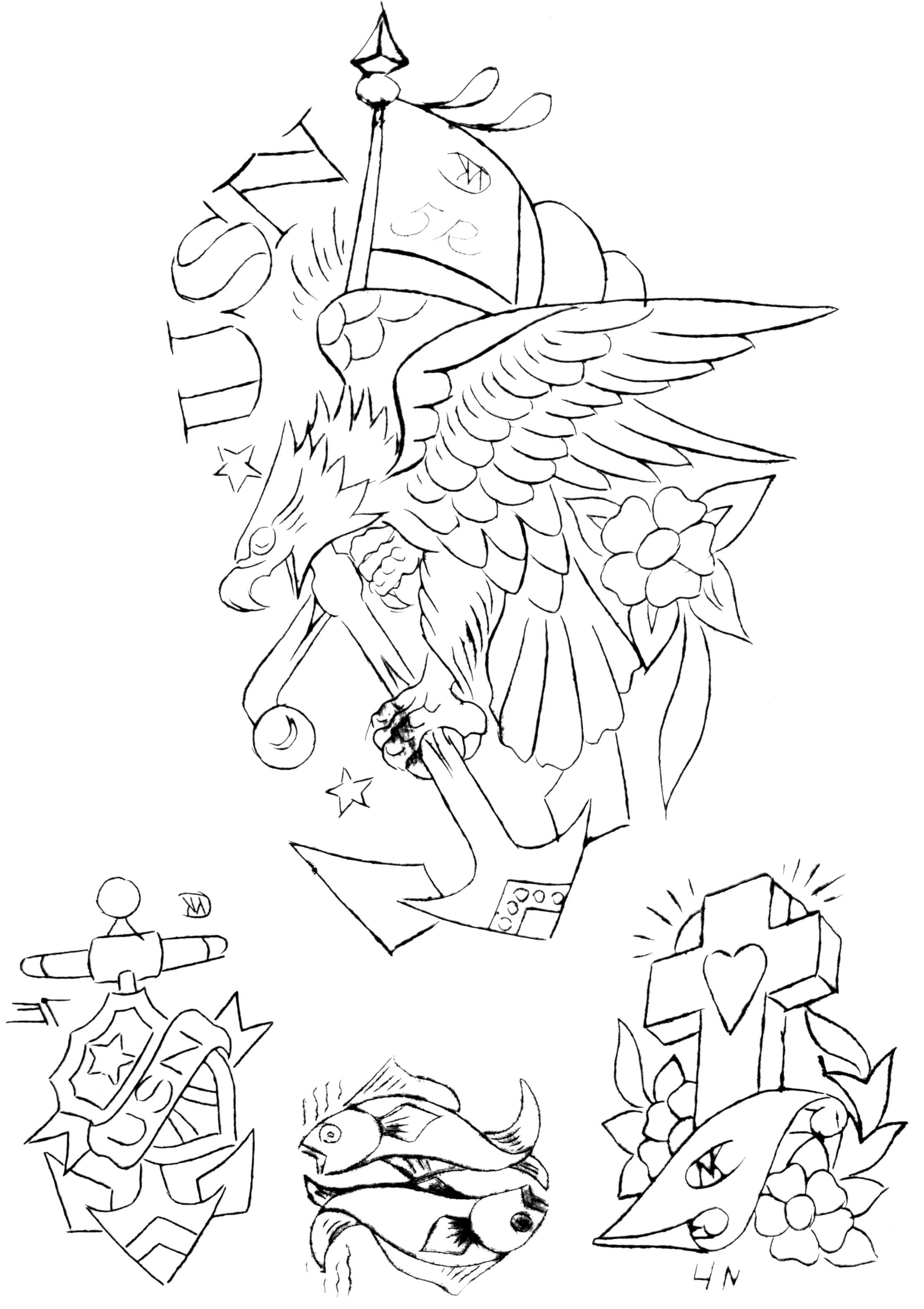

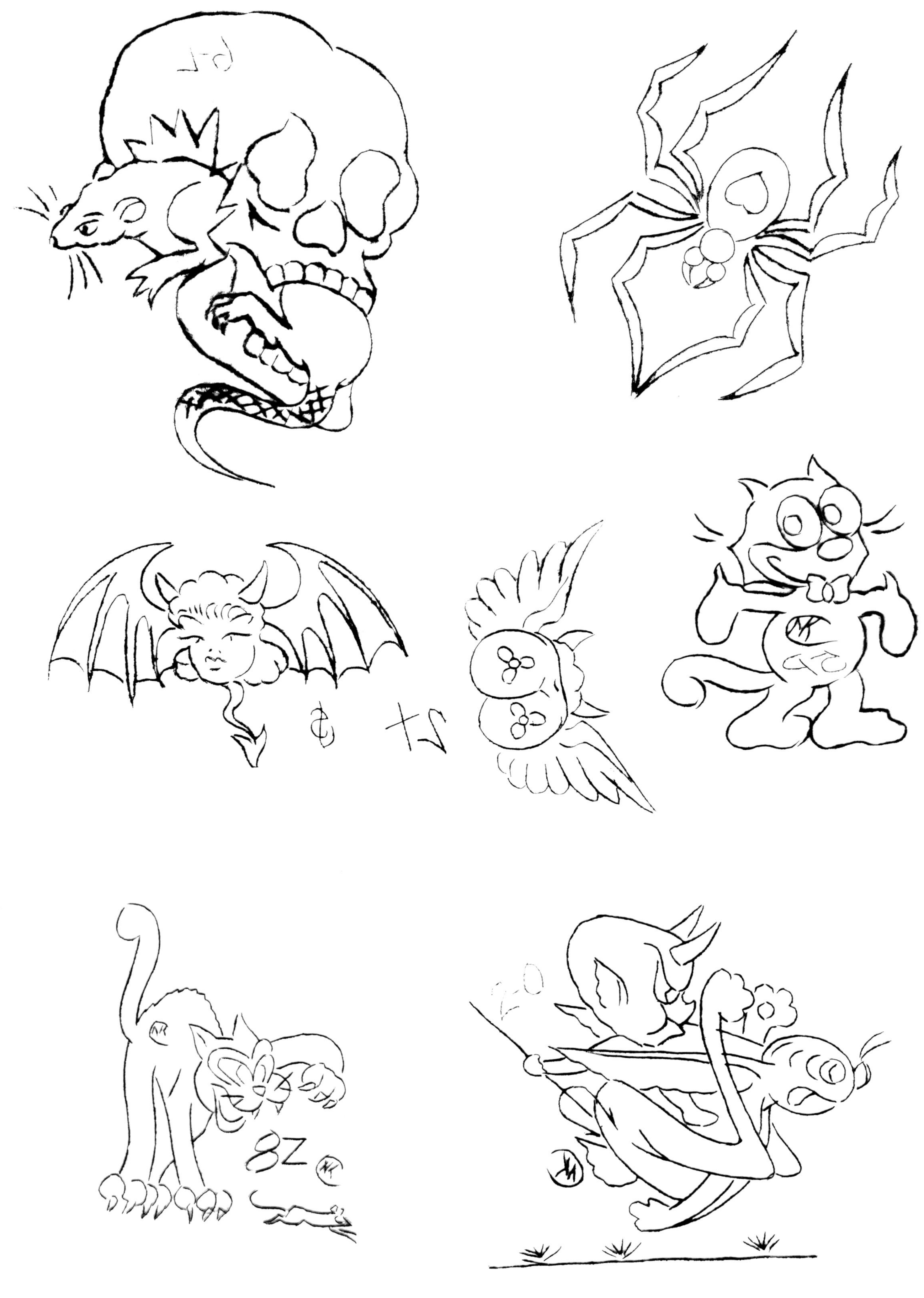

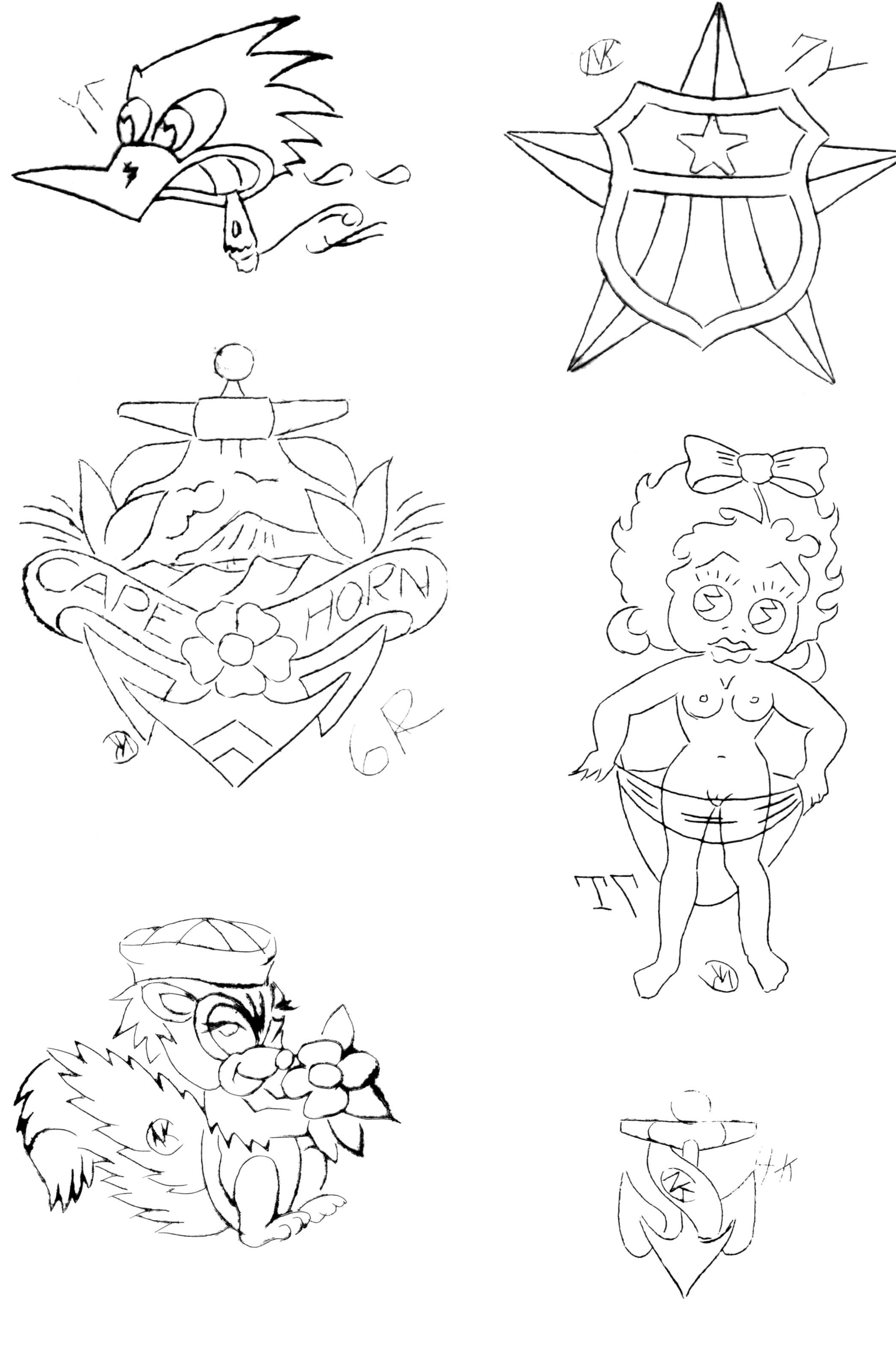
CAPE
HORN

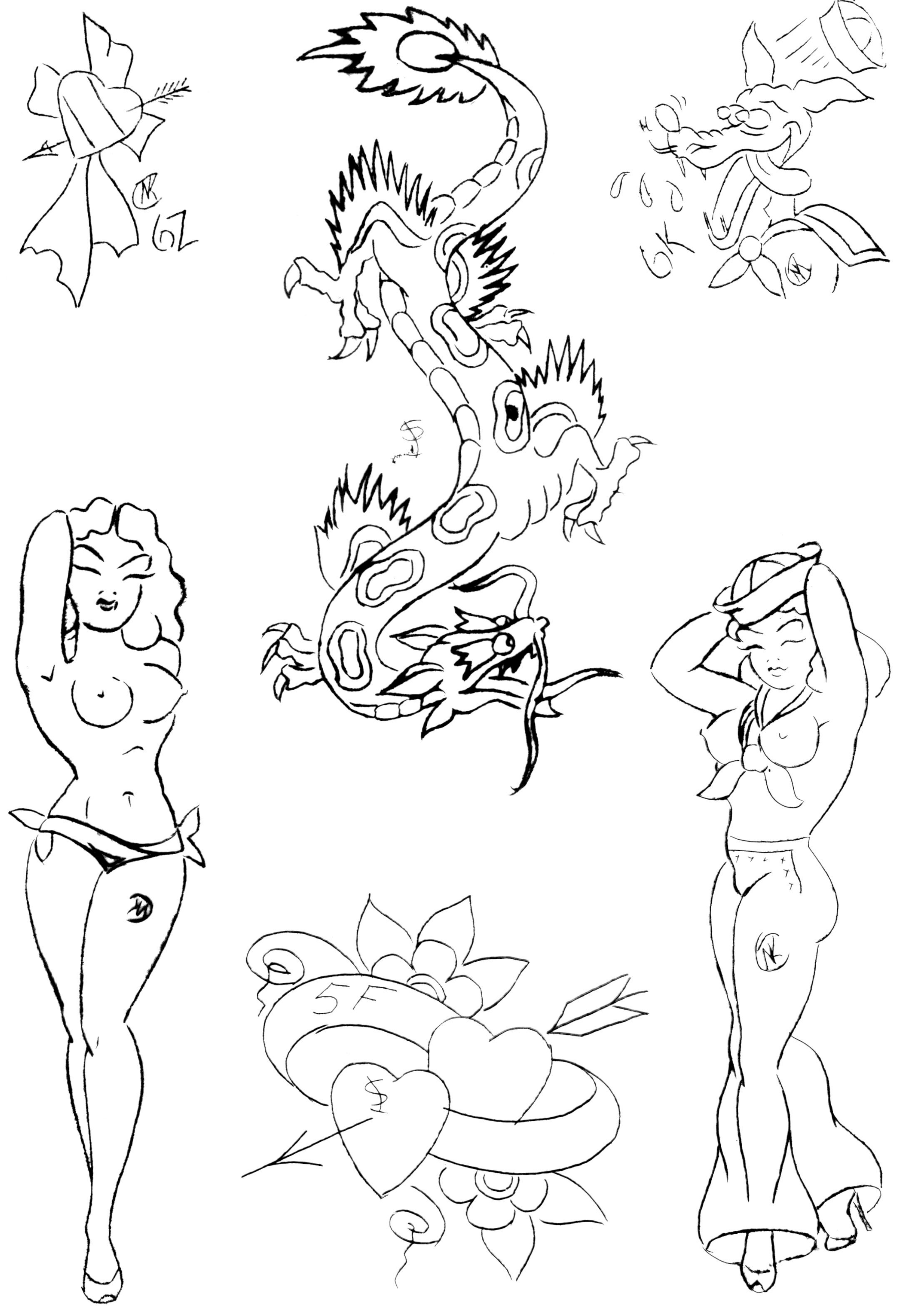

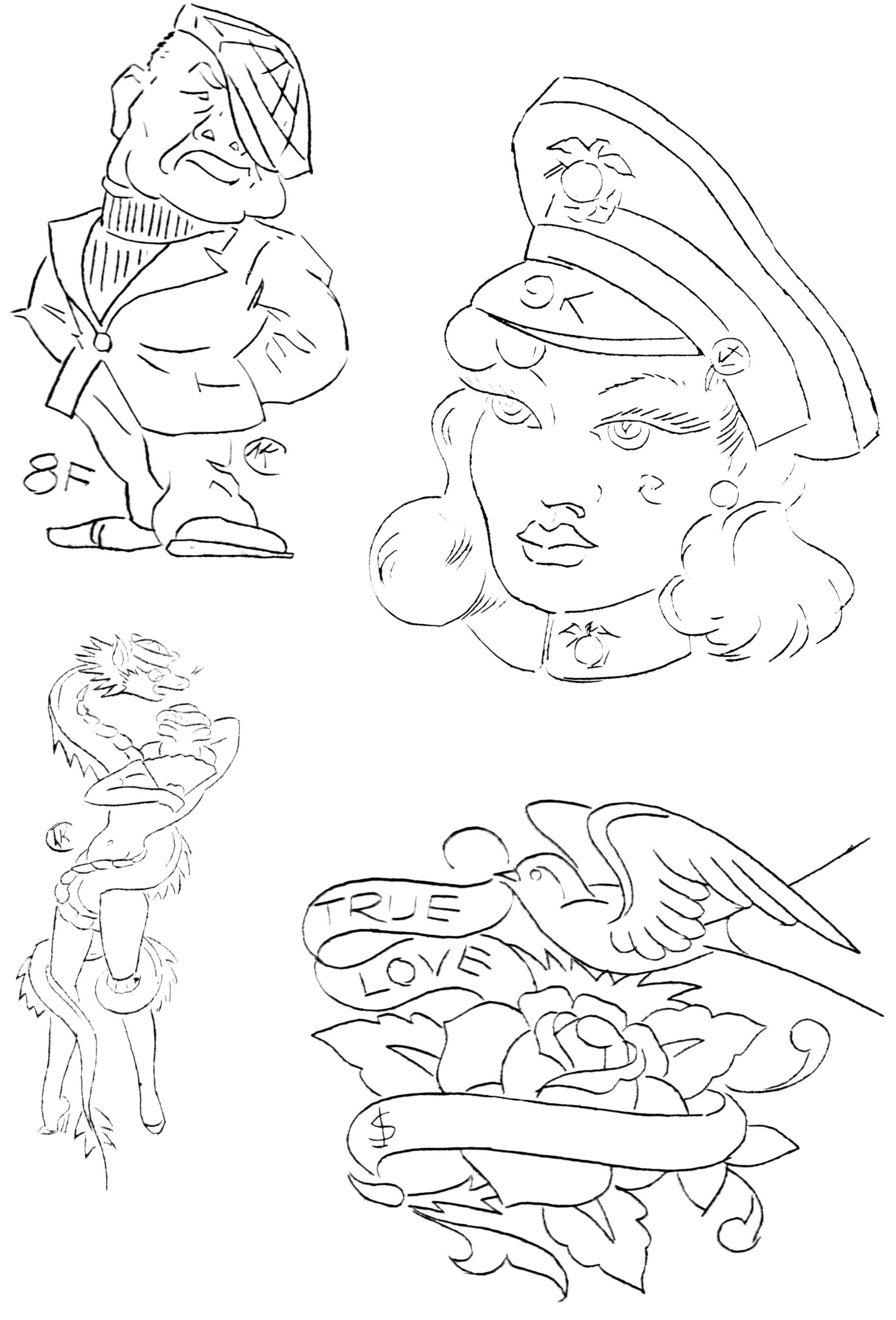

8F
9K
TRUE
LOVE
$

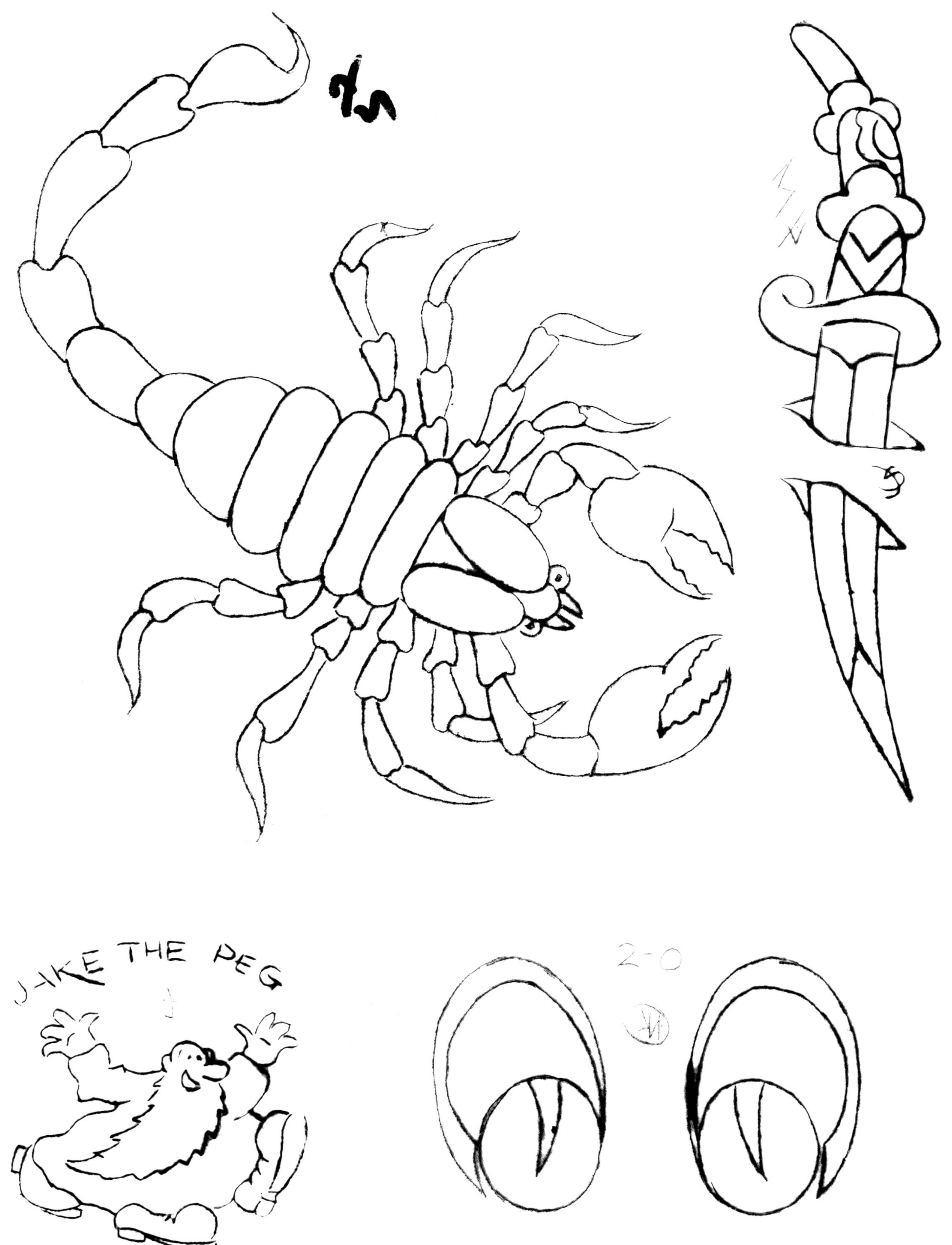
JAKE THE PEG
2-0

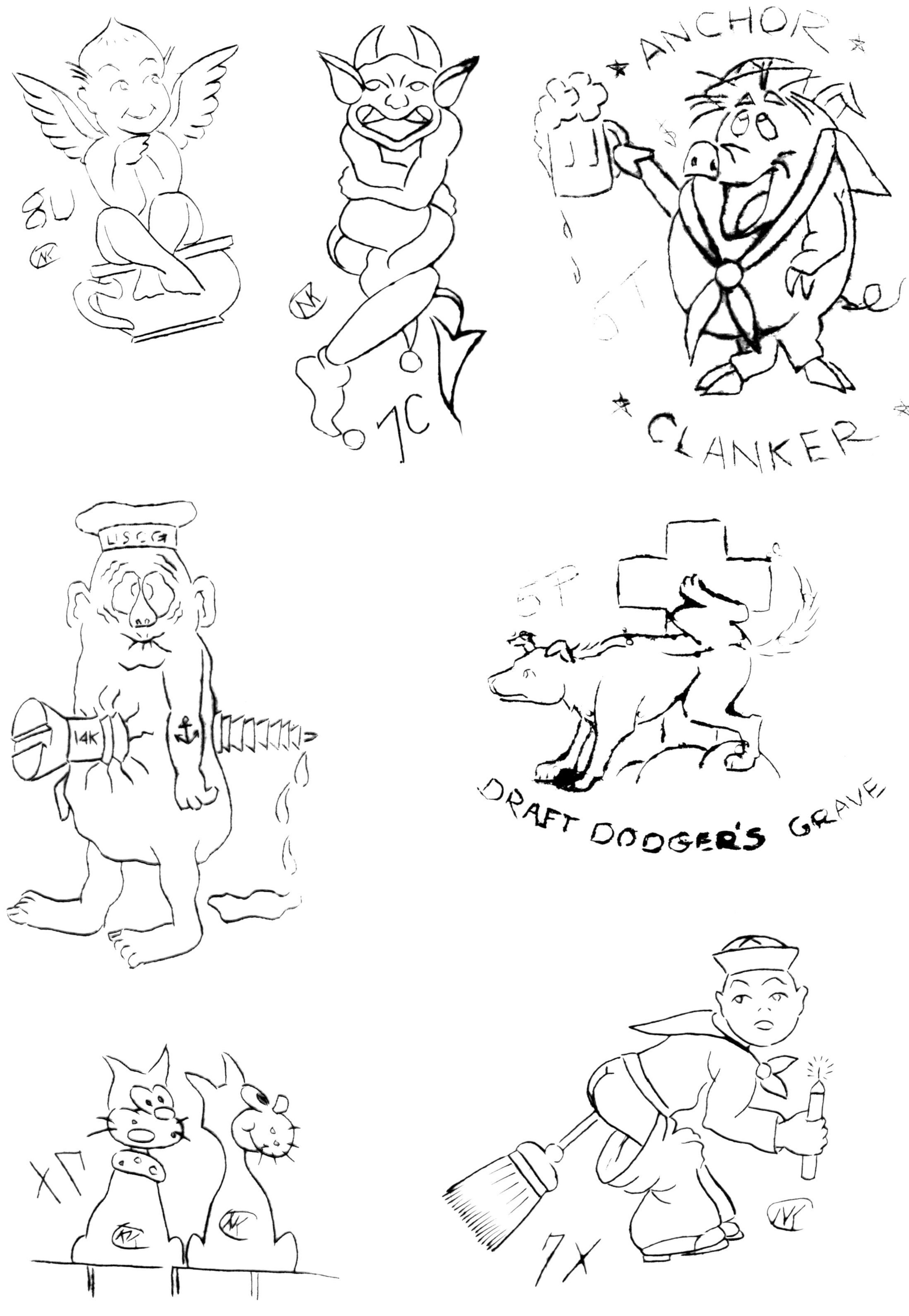
8U
7C
ANCHOR
5T
CLANKER
USCG
14K
5P
DRAFT DODGER'S GRAVE
7X

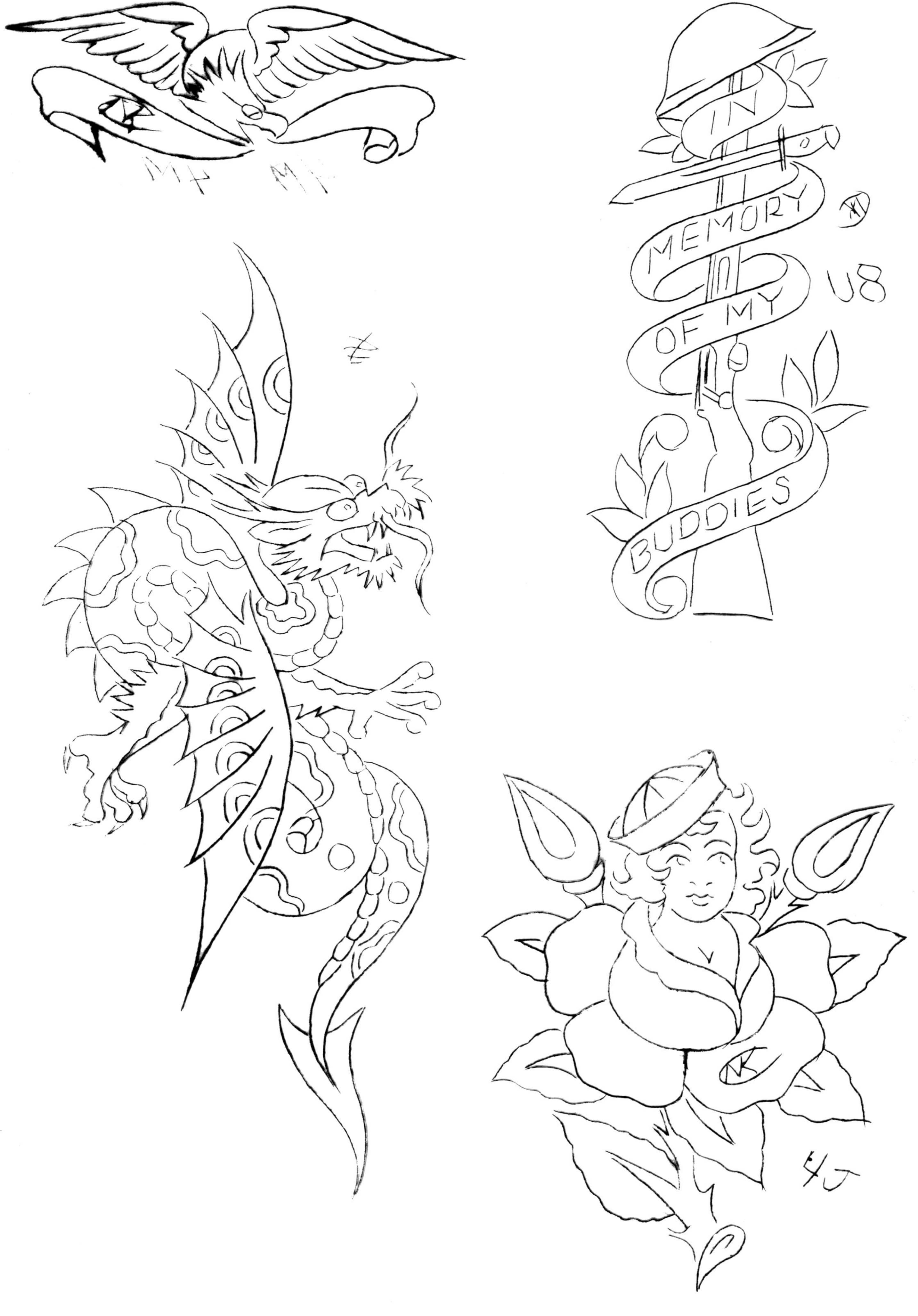

IN
MEMORY
OF MY
BUDDIES

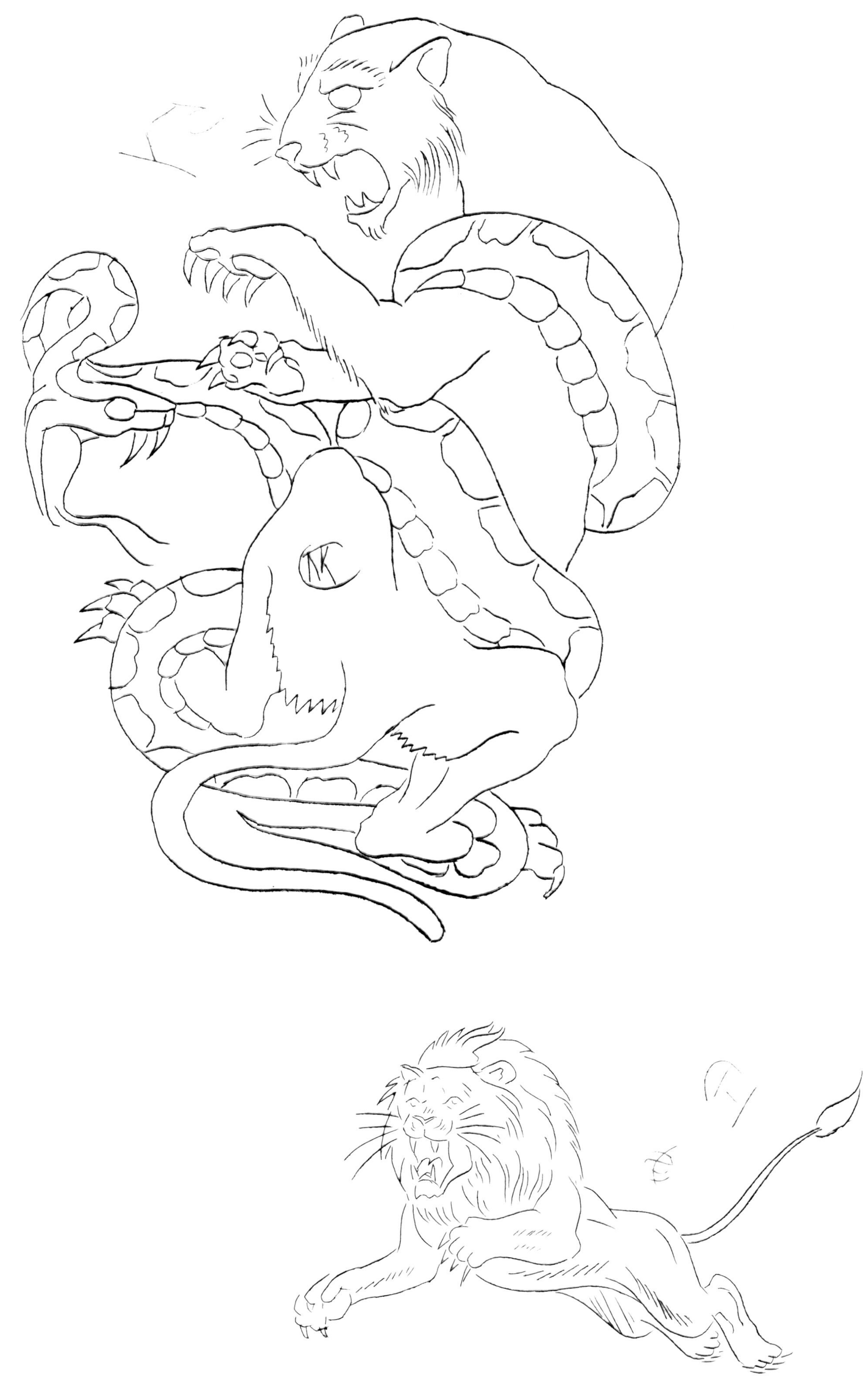

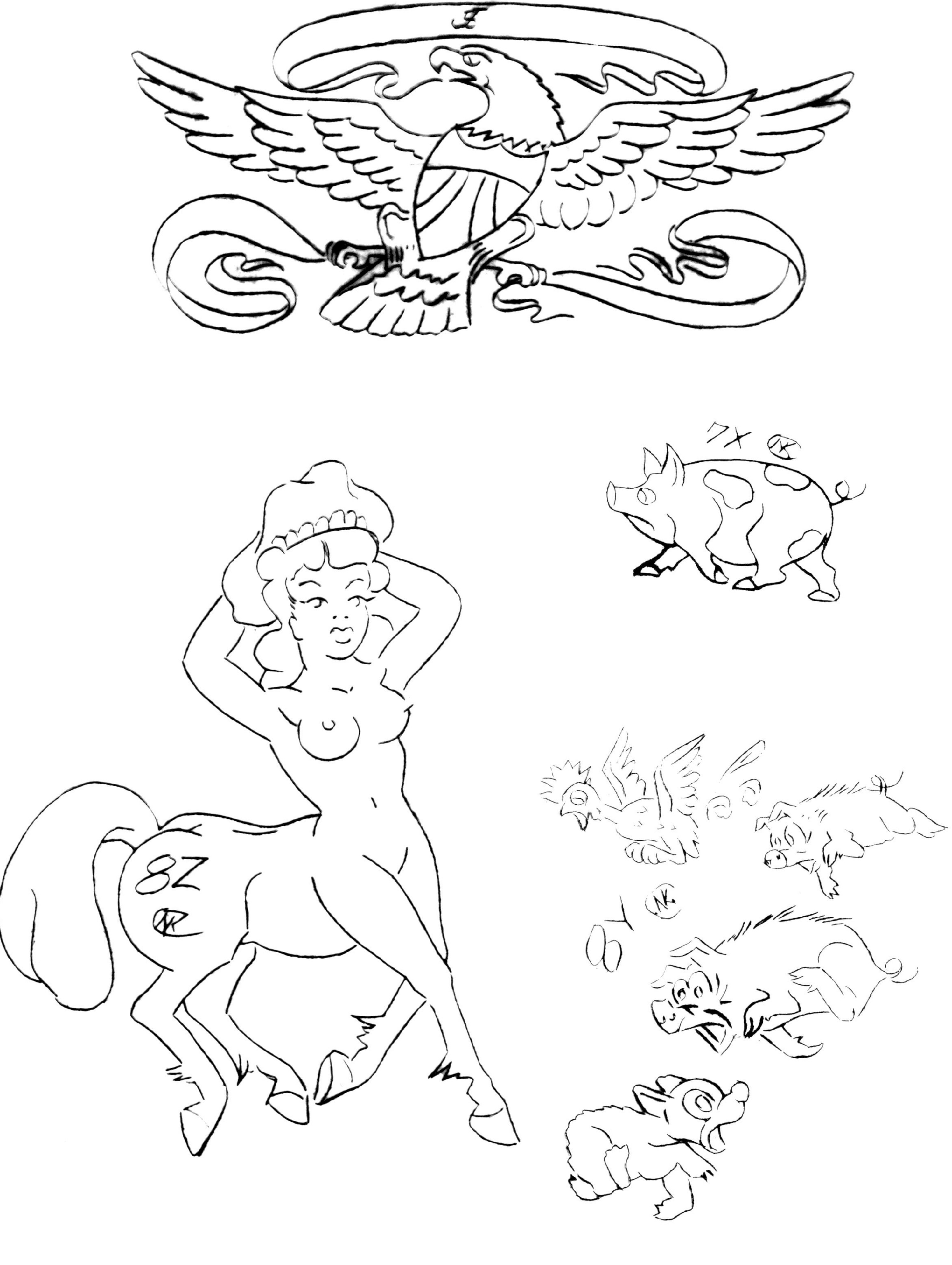
8Z

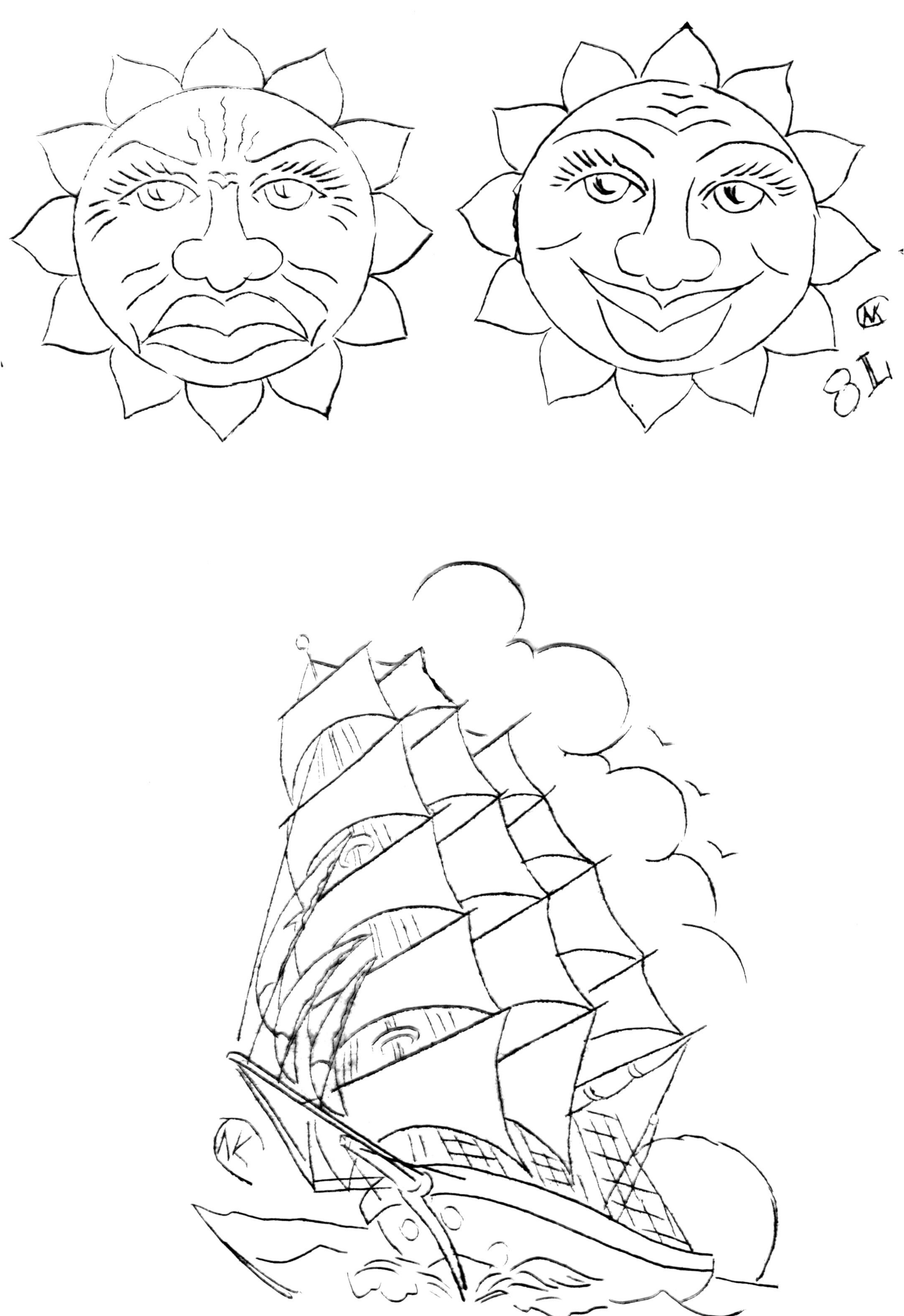

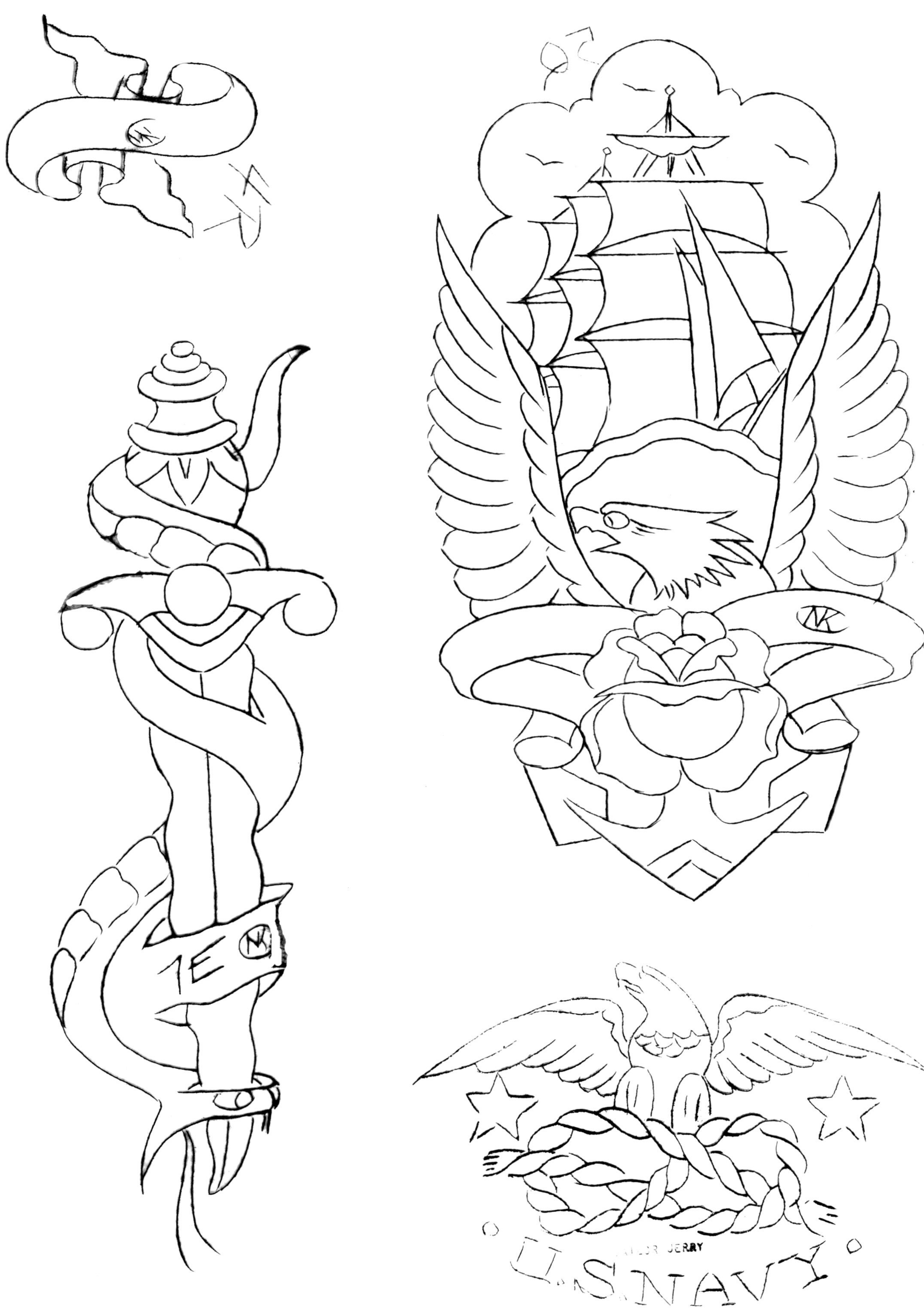
U.S.NAVY

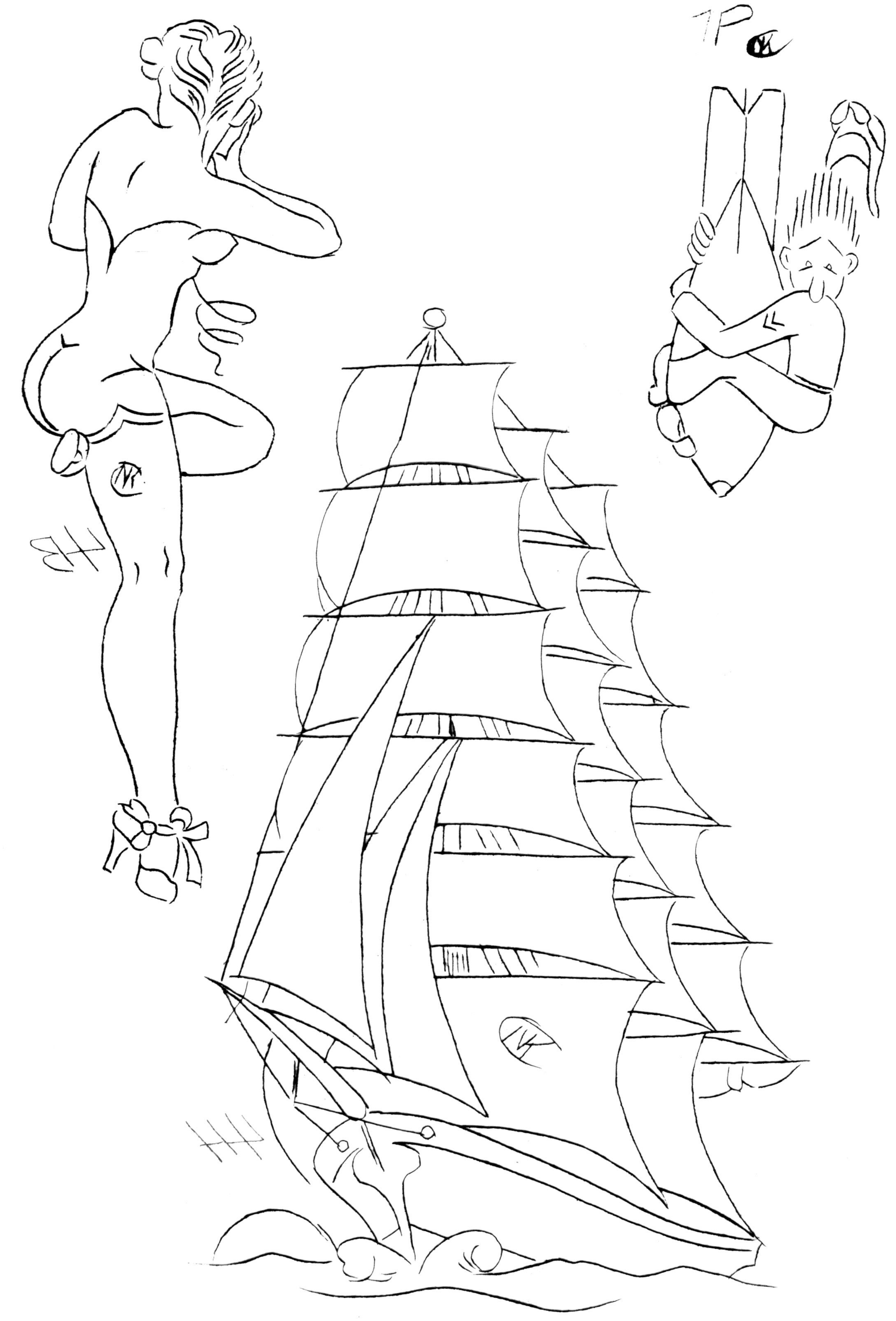

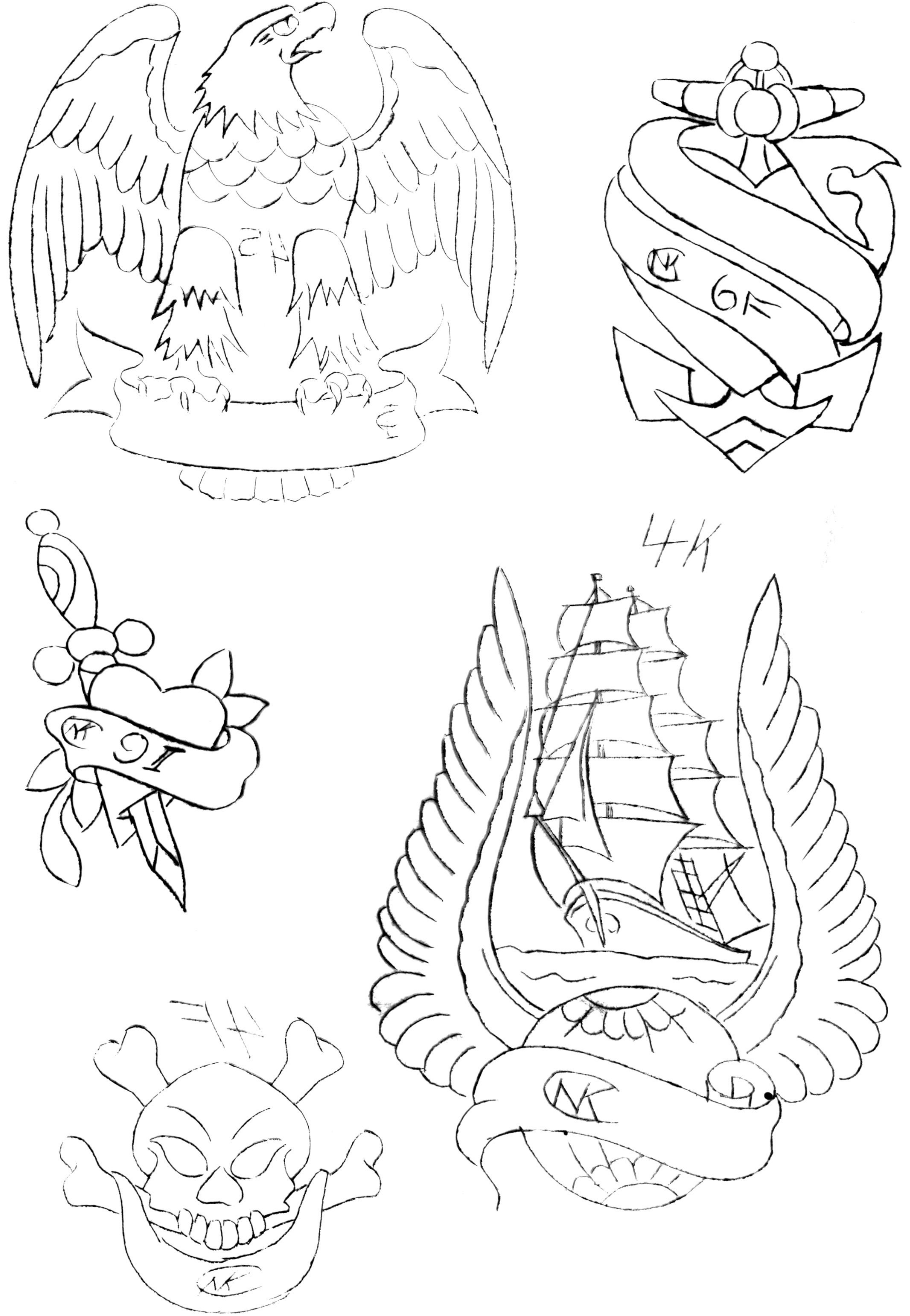

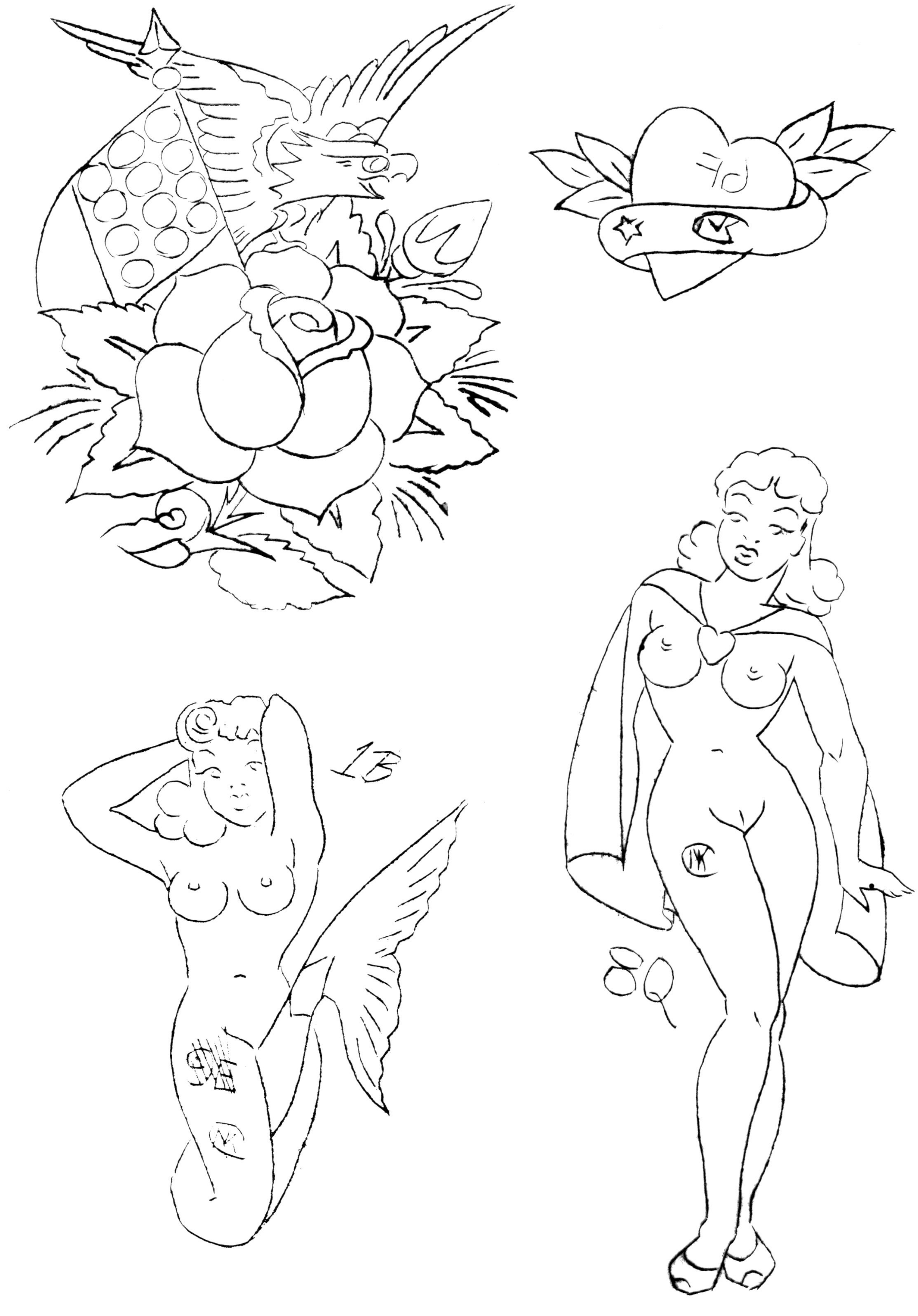

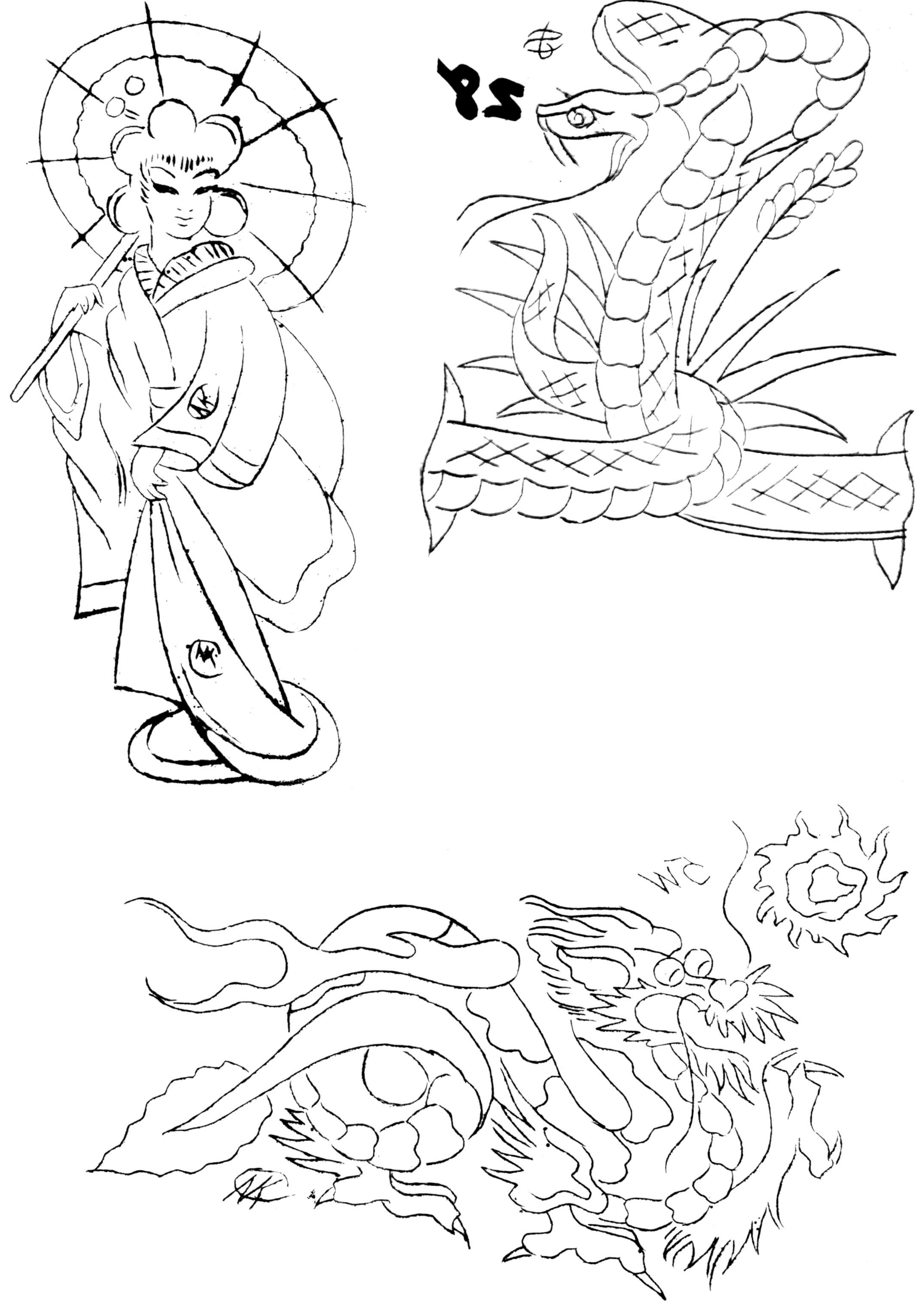

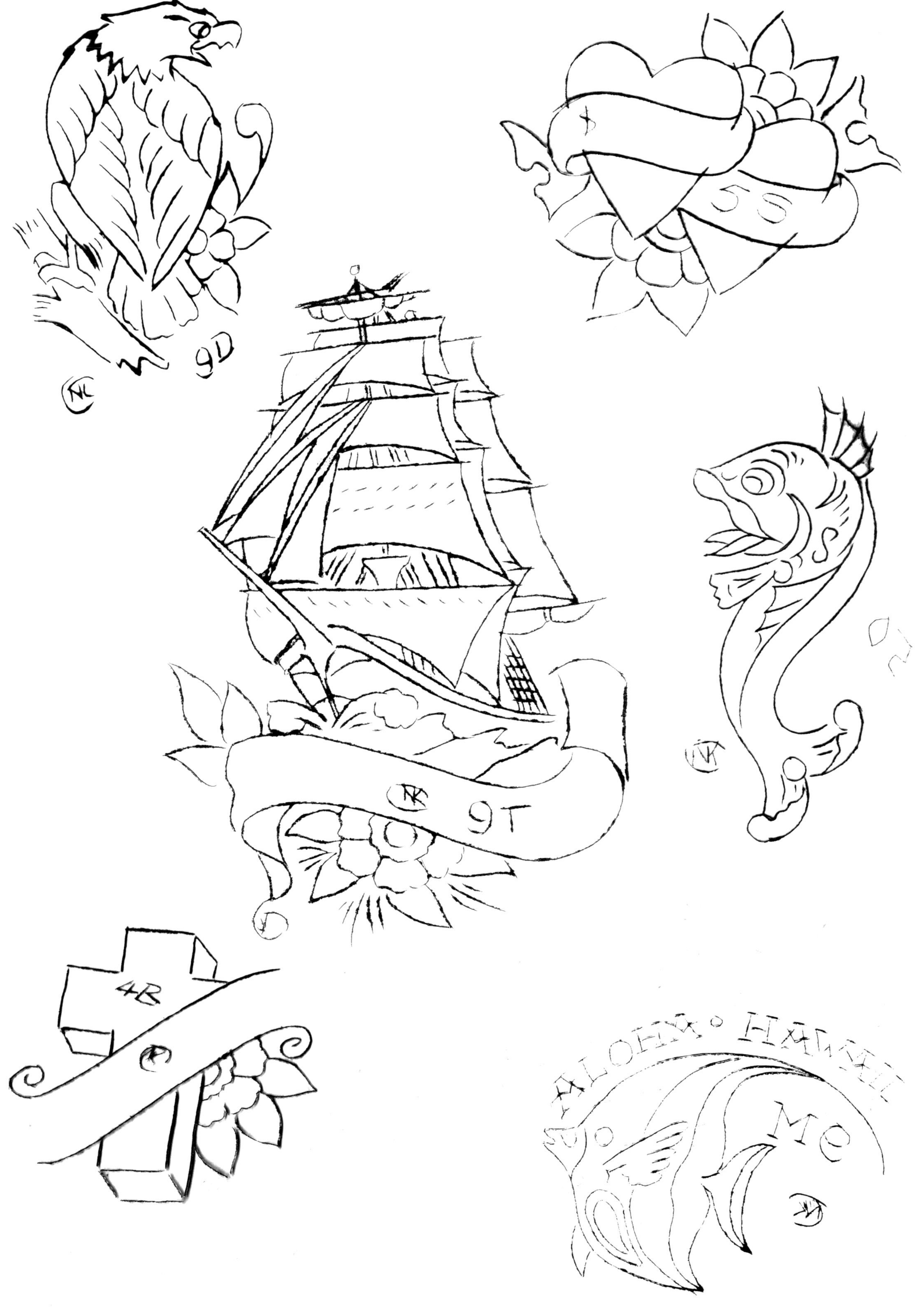
9D
5S
9T
4B
ALOHA • HAWAII
MO

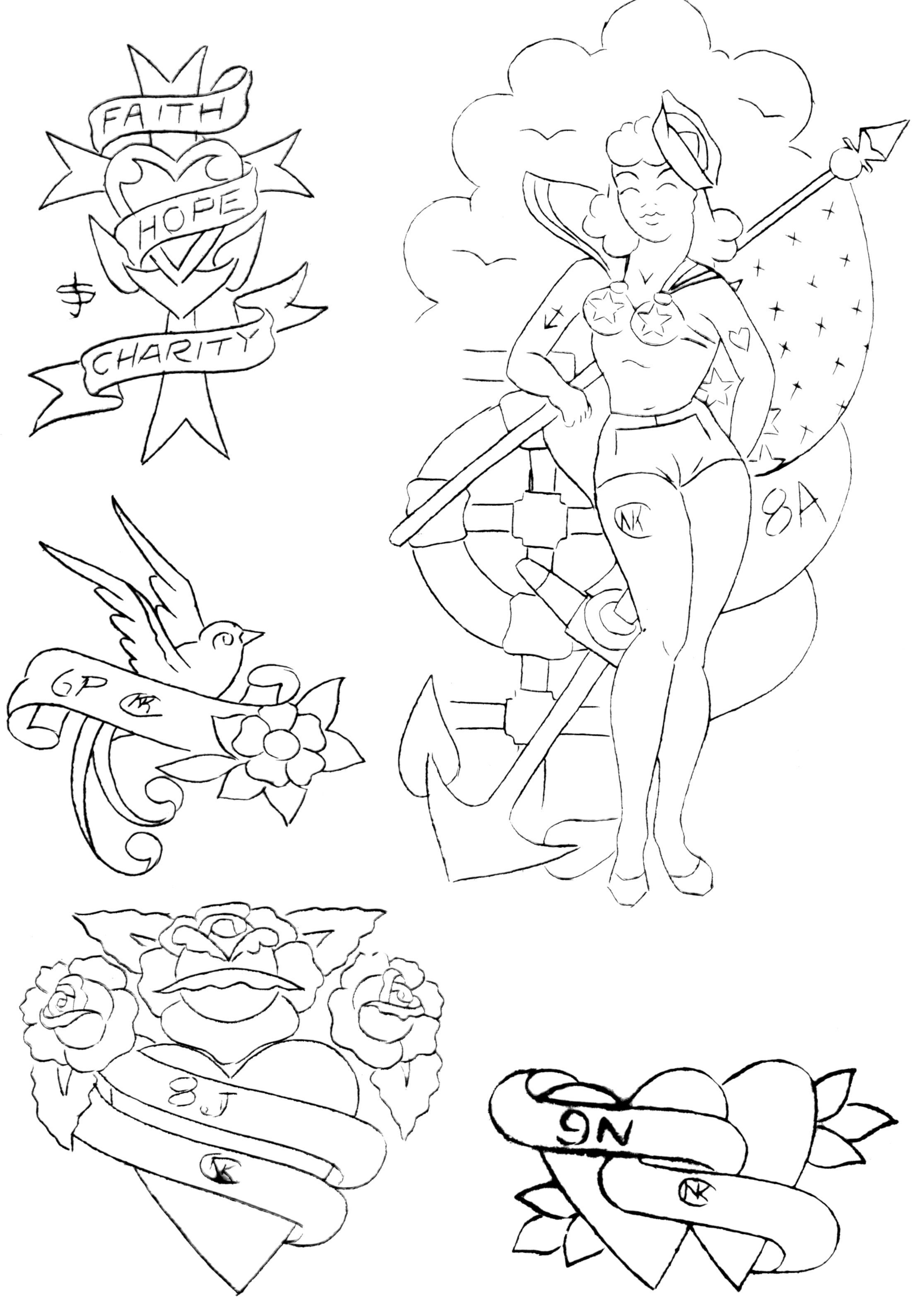
FAITH
HOPE
CHARITY
8A
GP
8J
9N

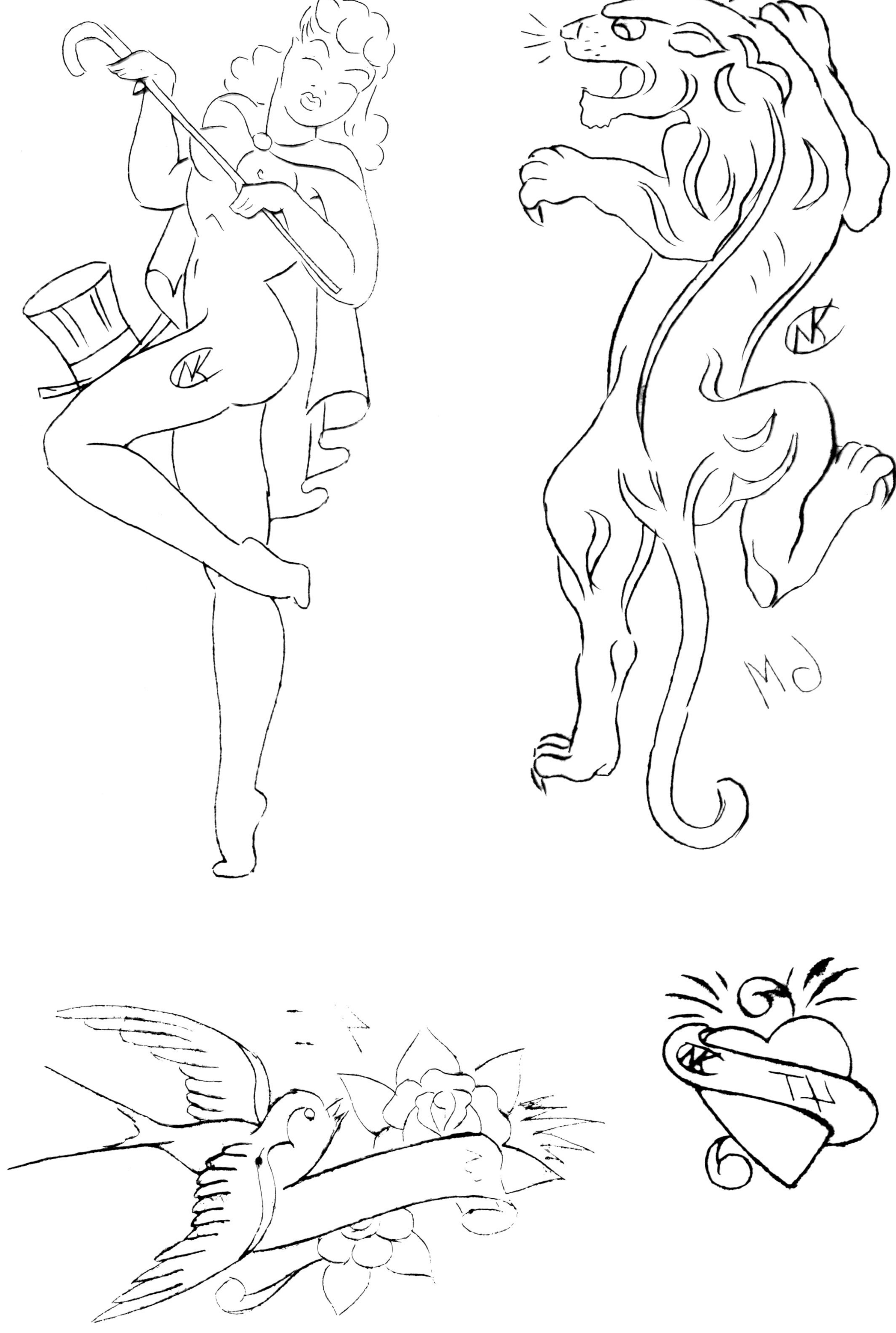

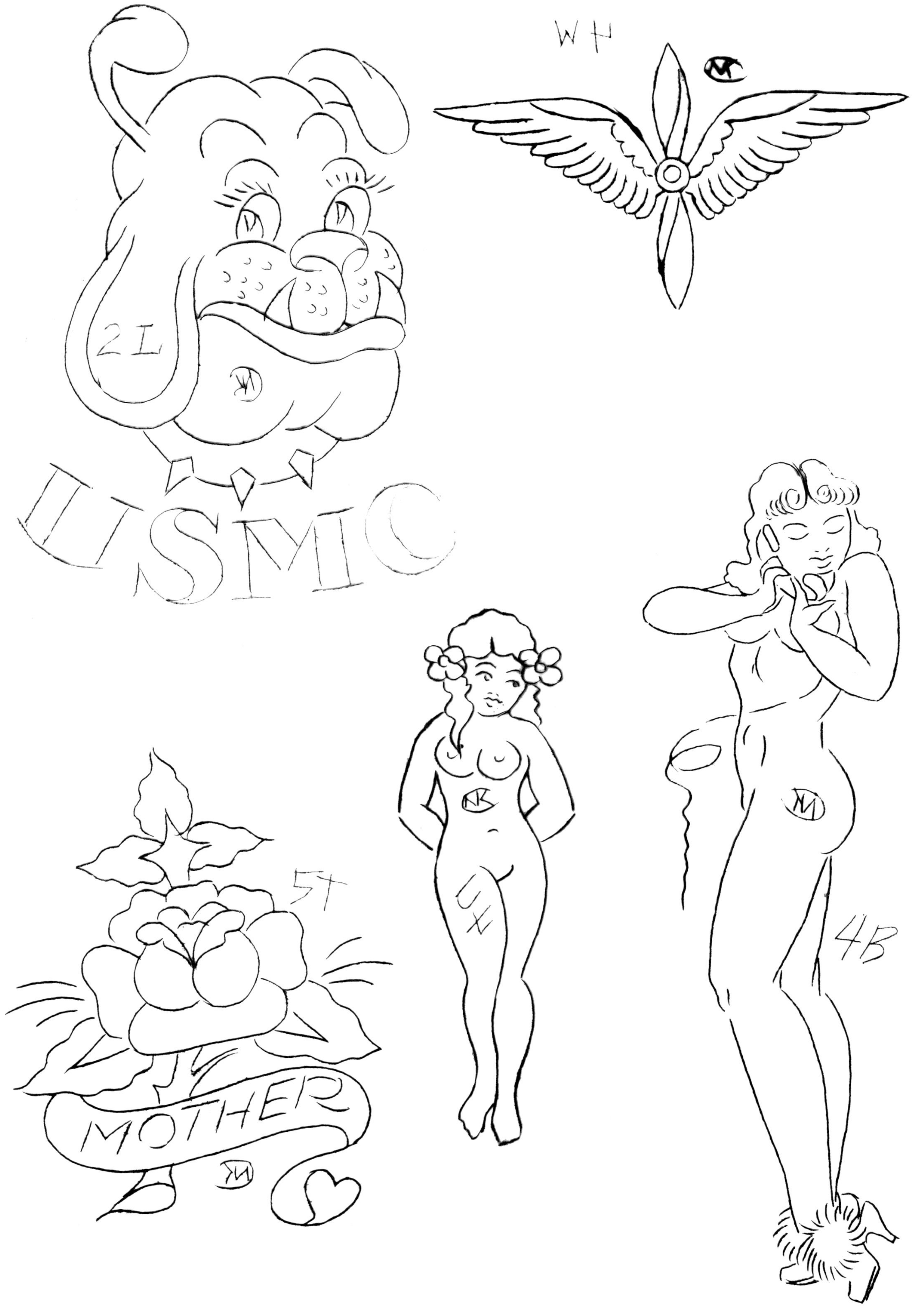

WH
21
USMC
5T
MOTHER
4B

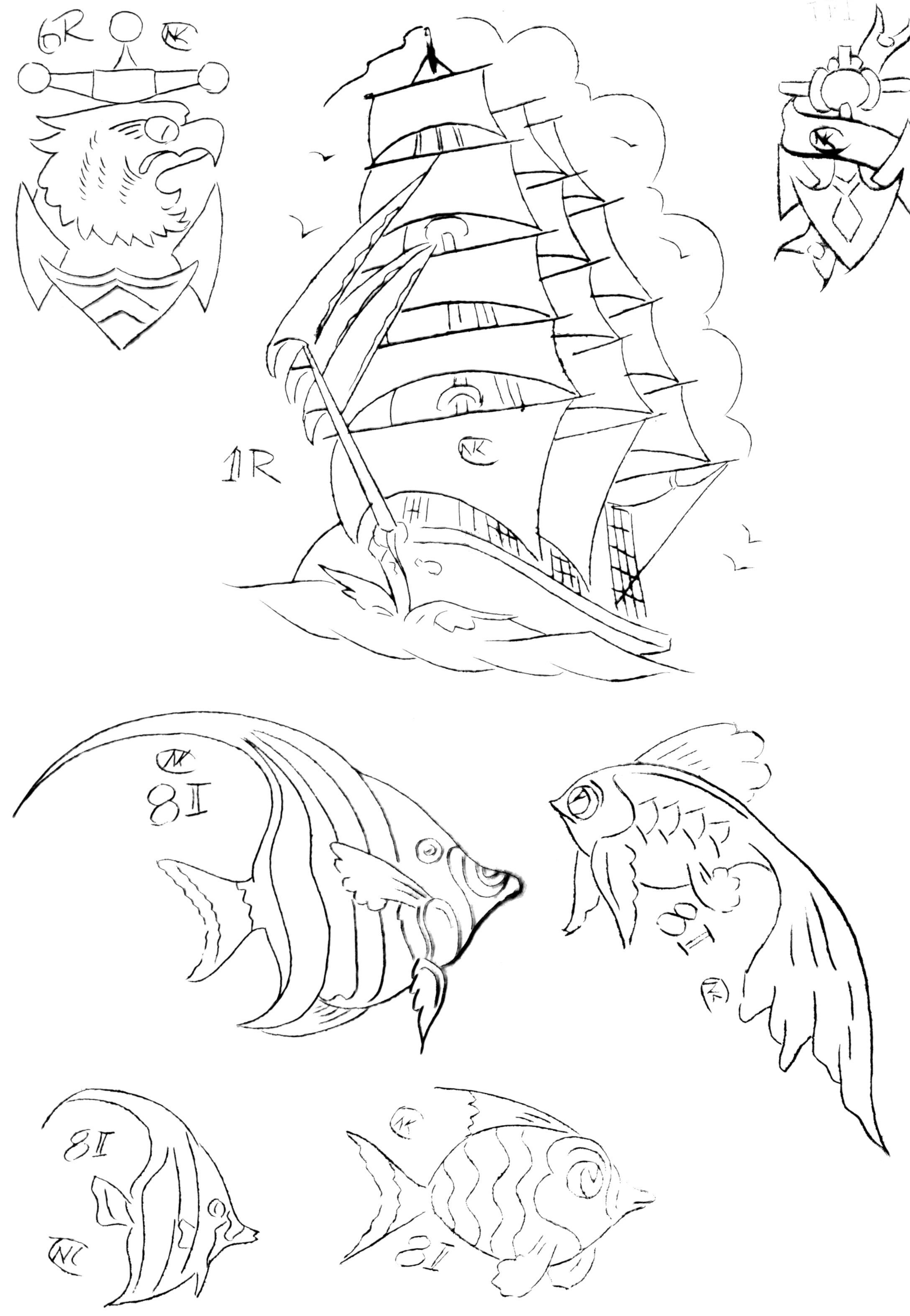

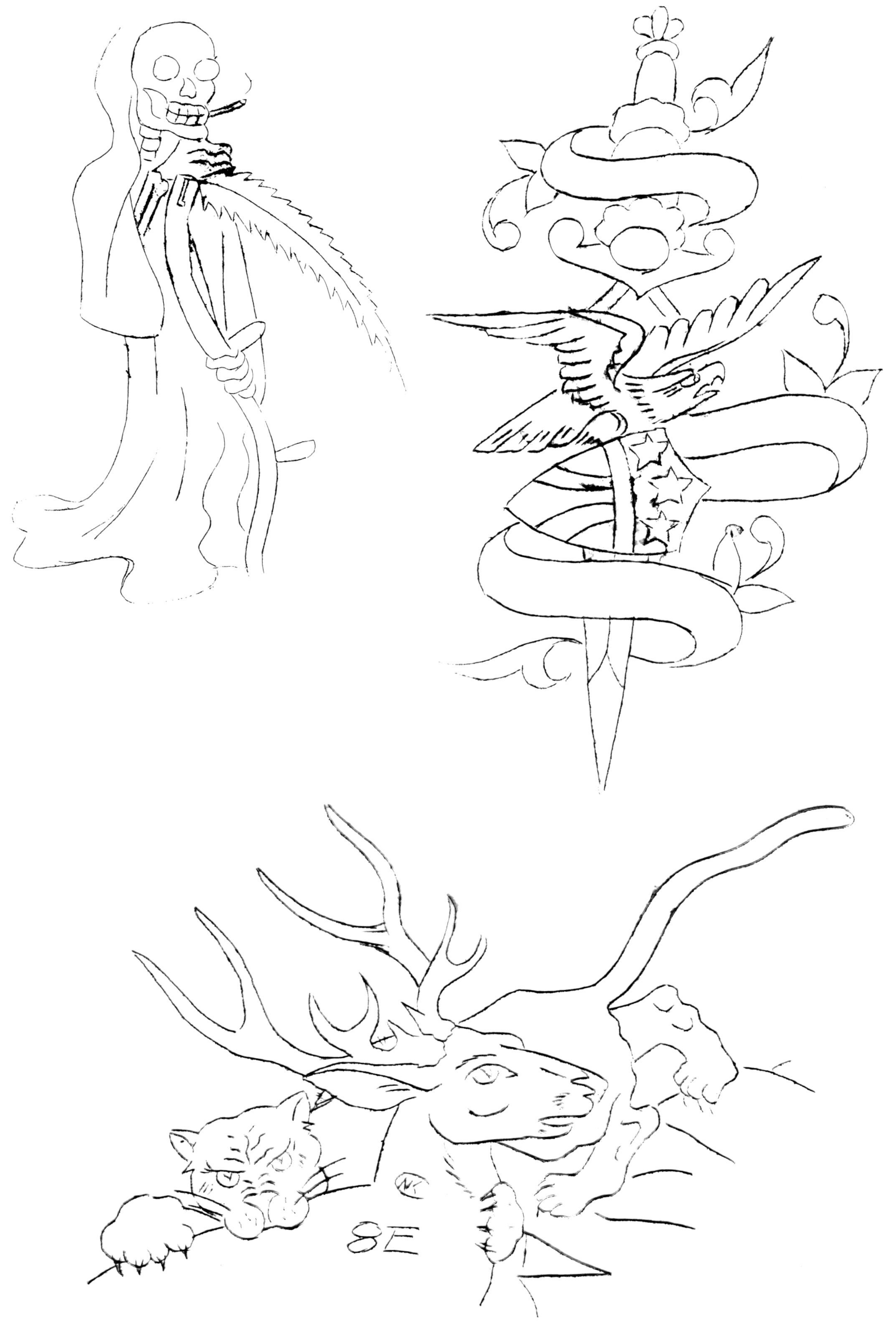
8E

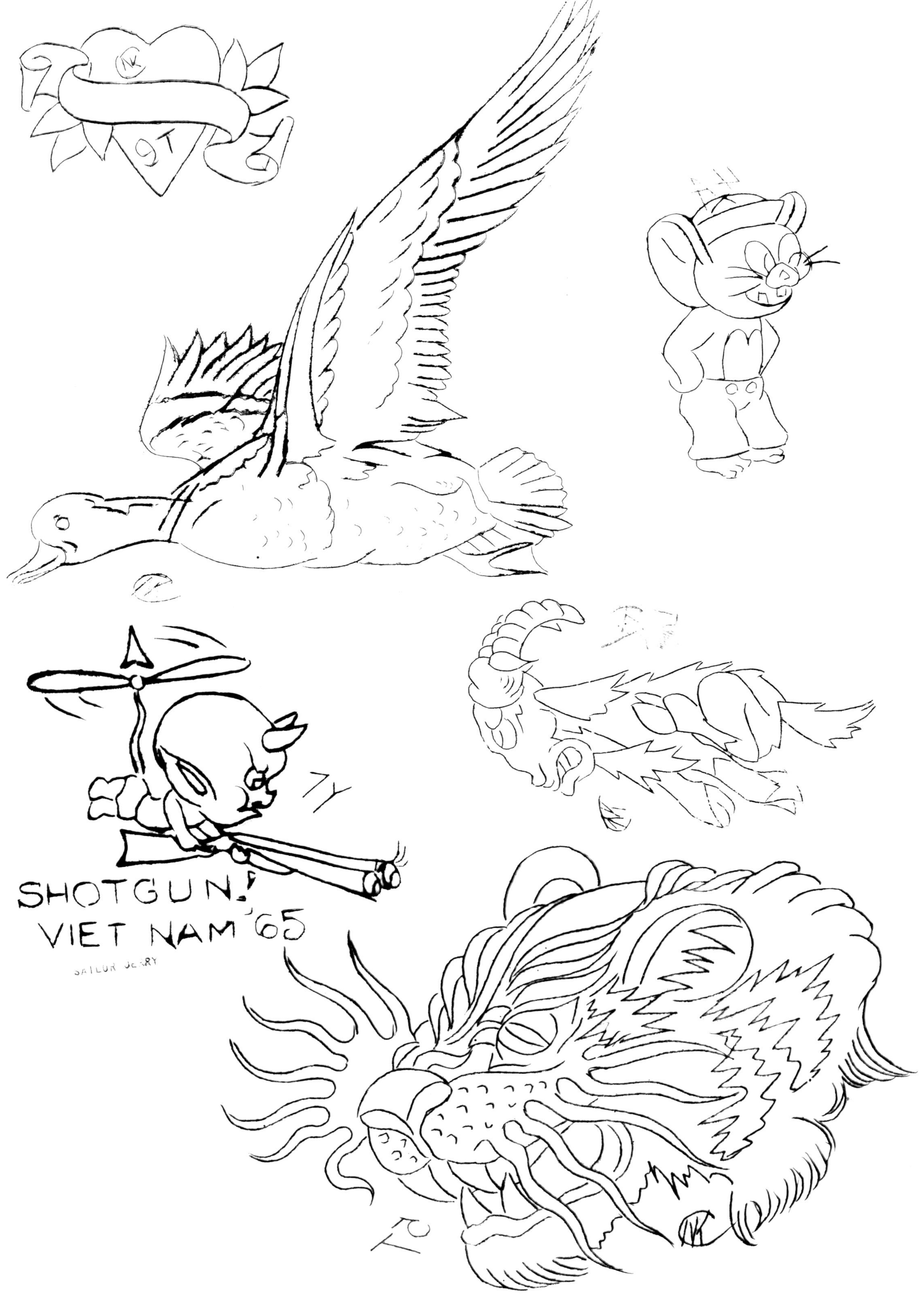
SHOTGUN!
VIET NAM '65
SAILOR JERRY

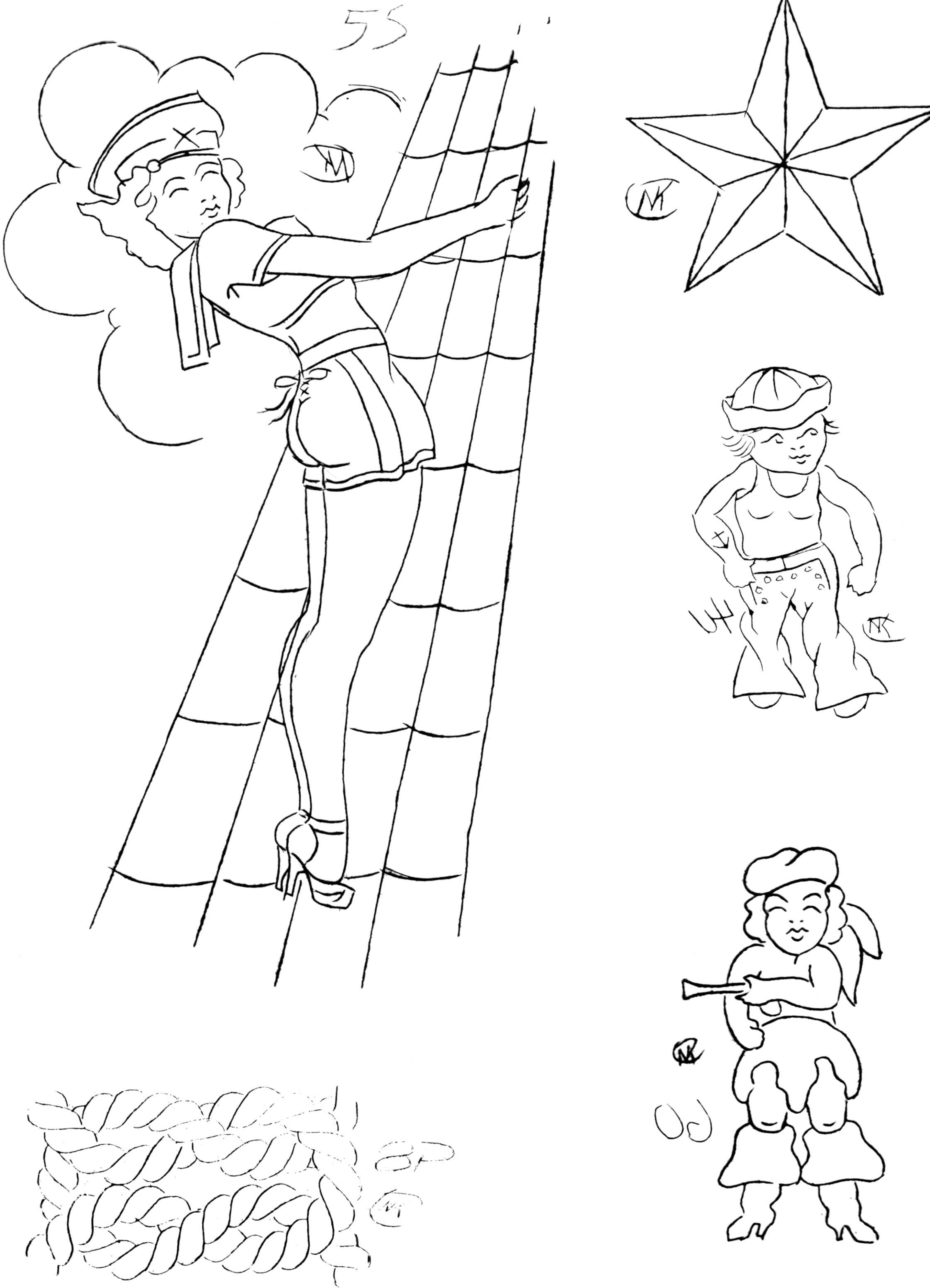

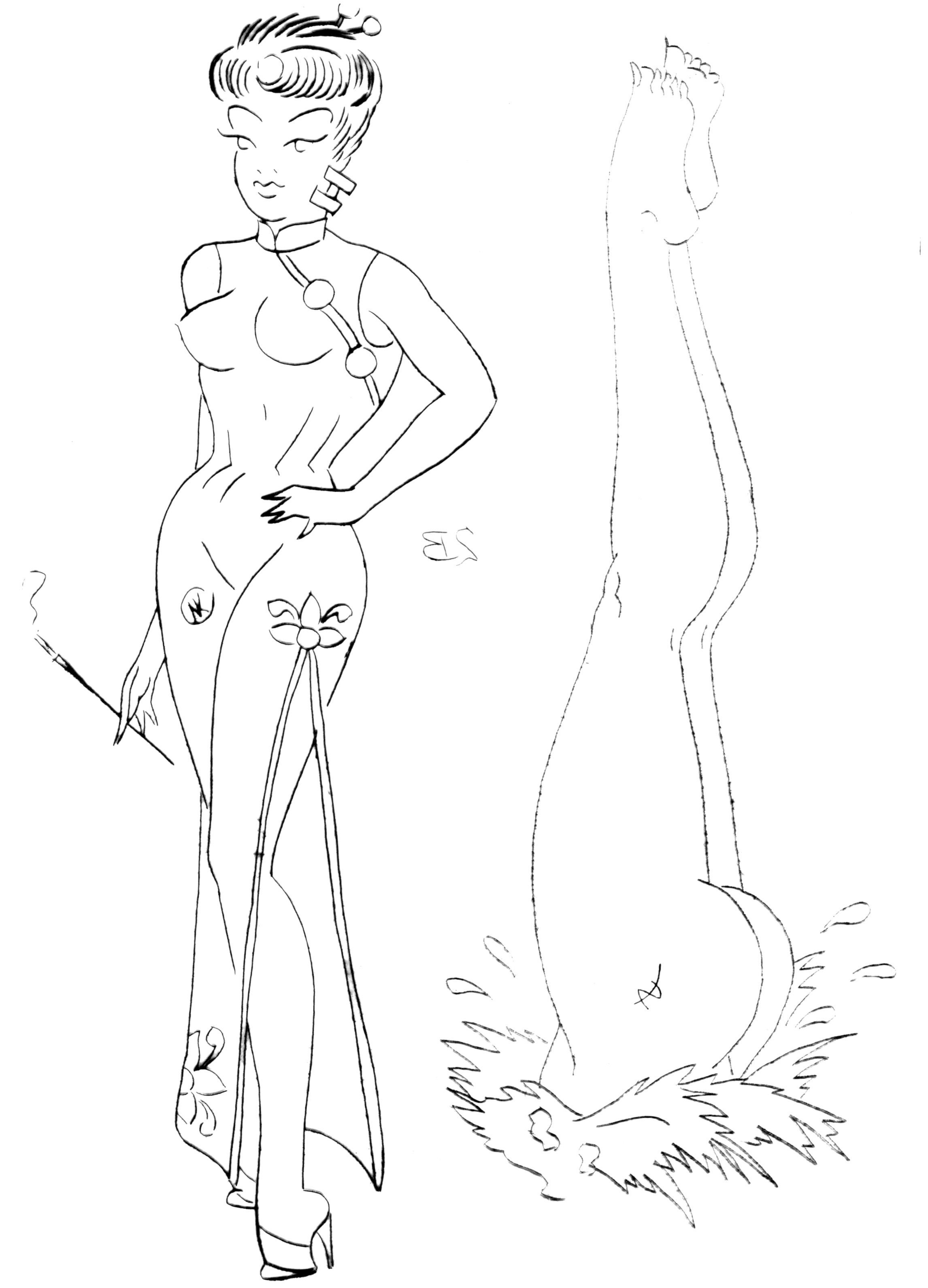

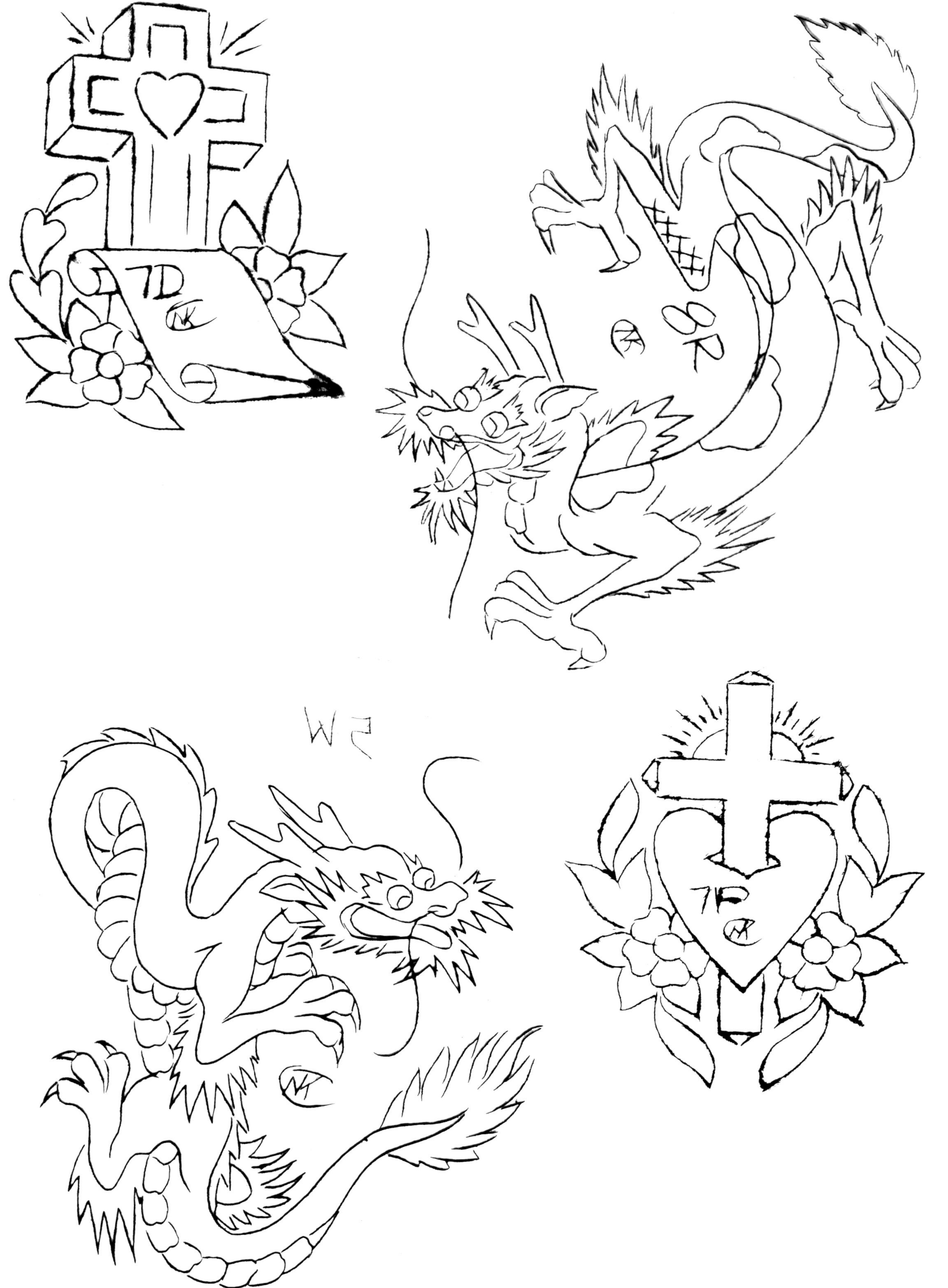

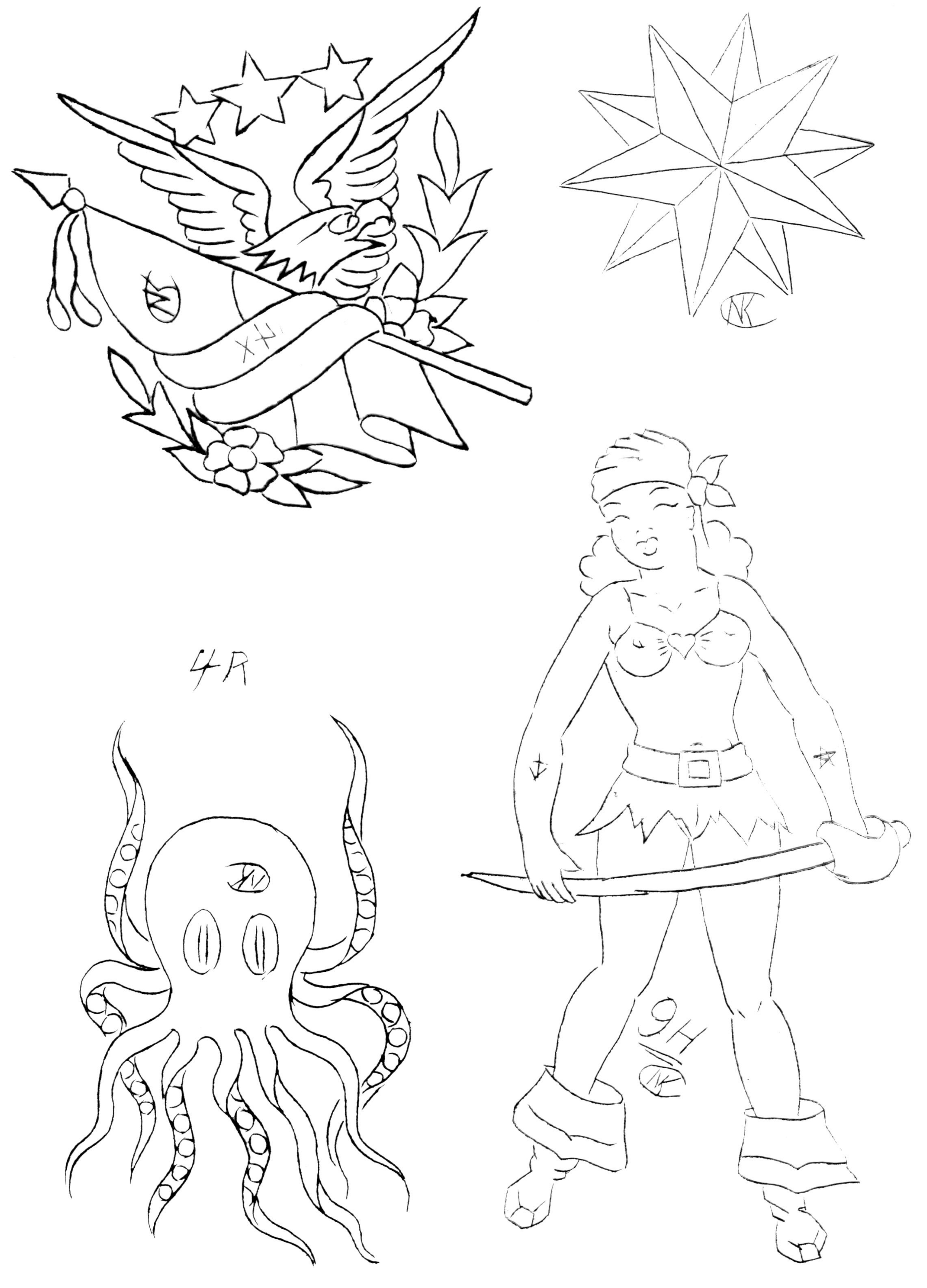

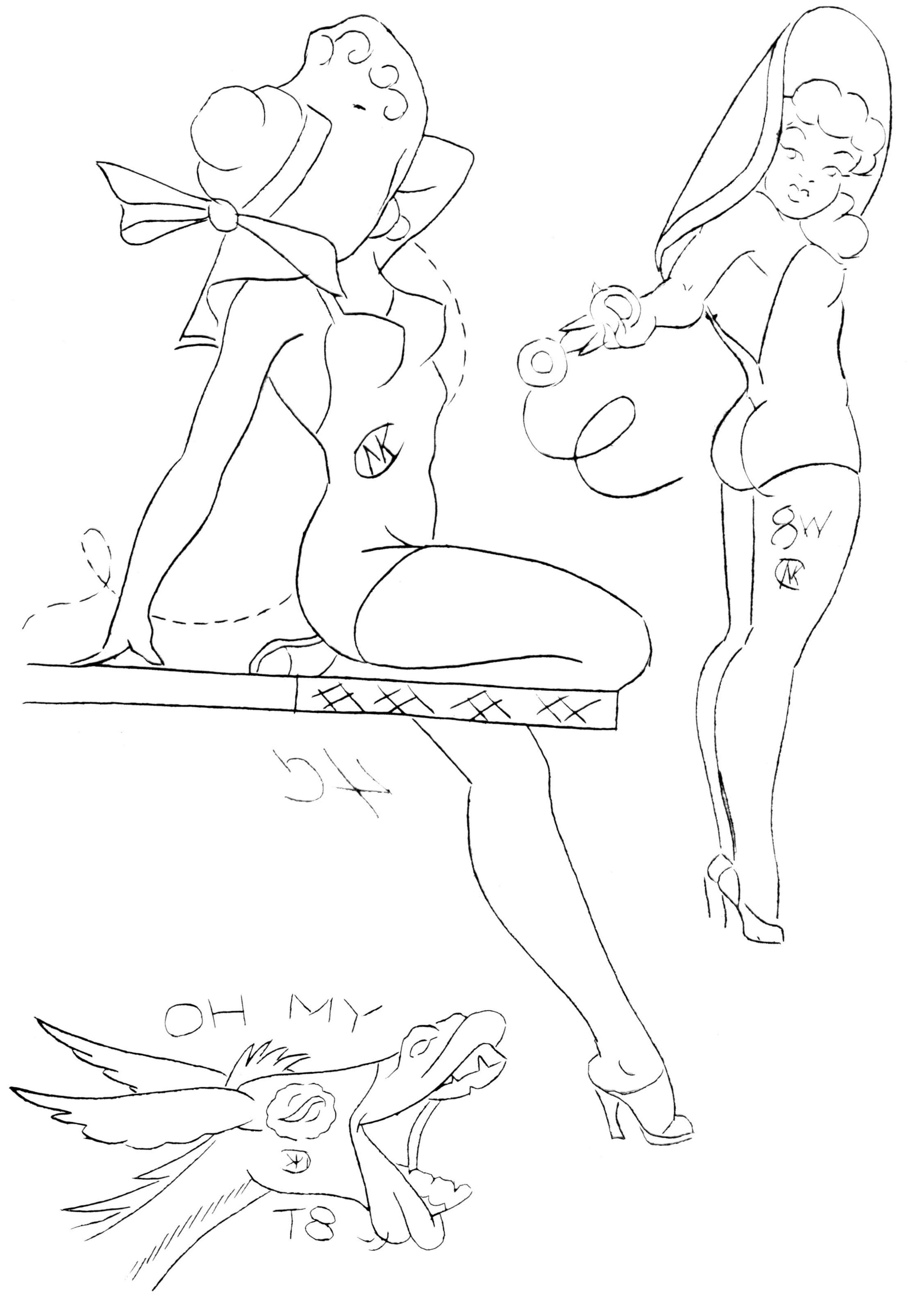
OH MY-
T8

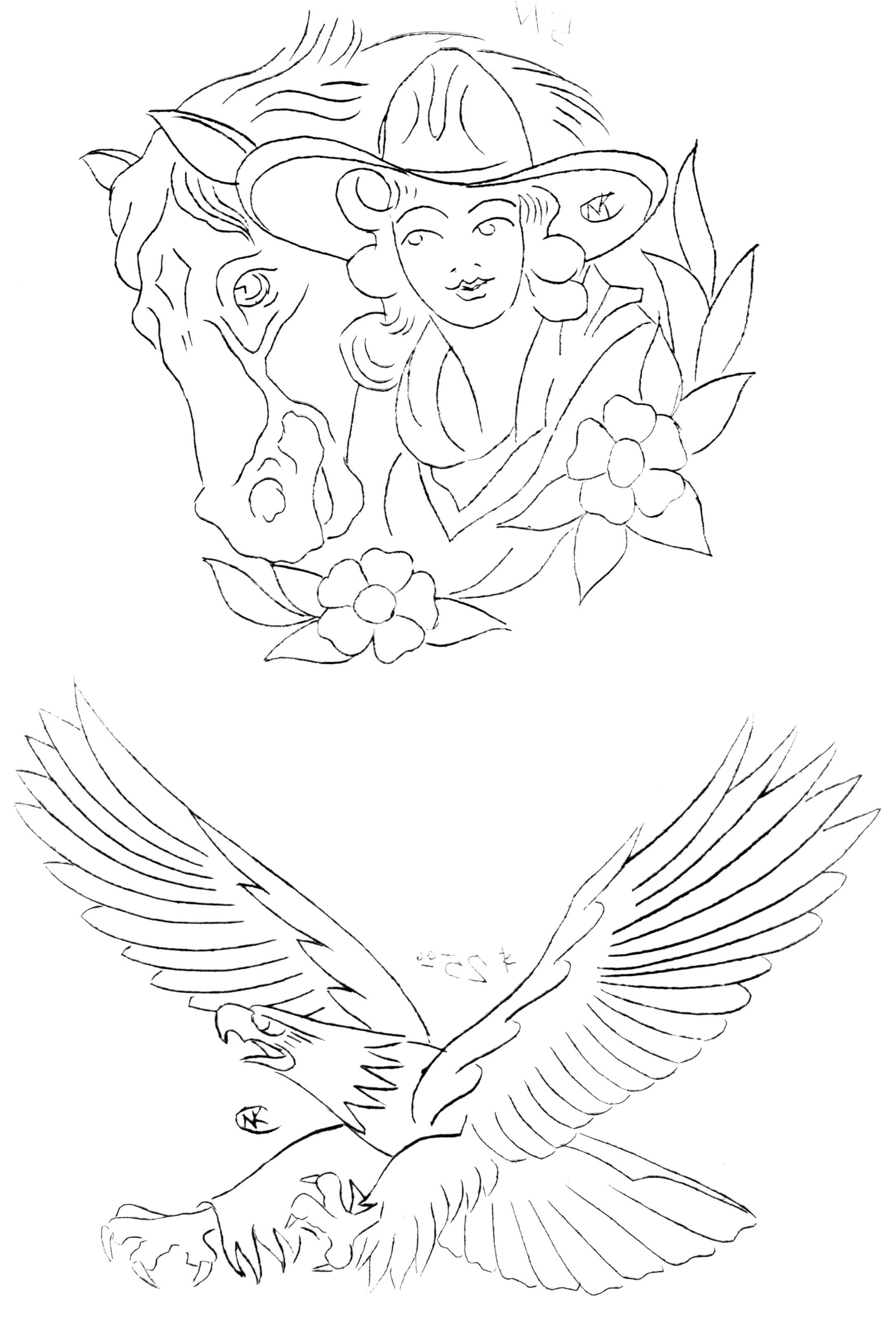

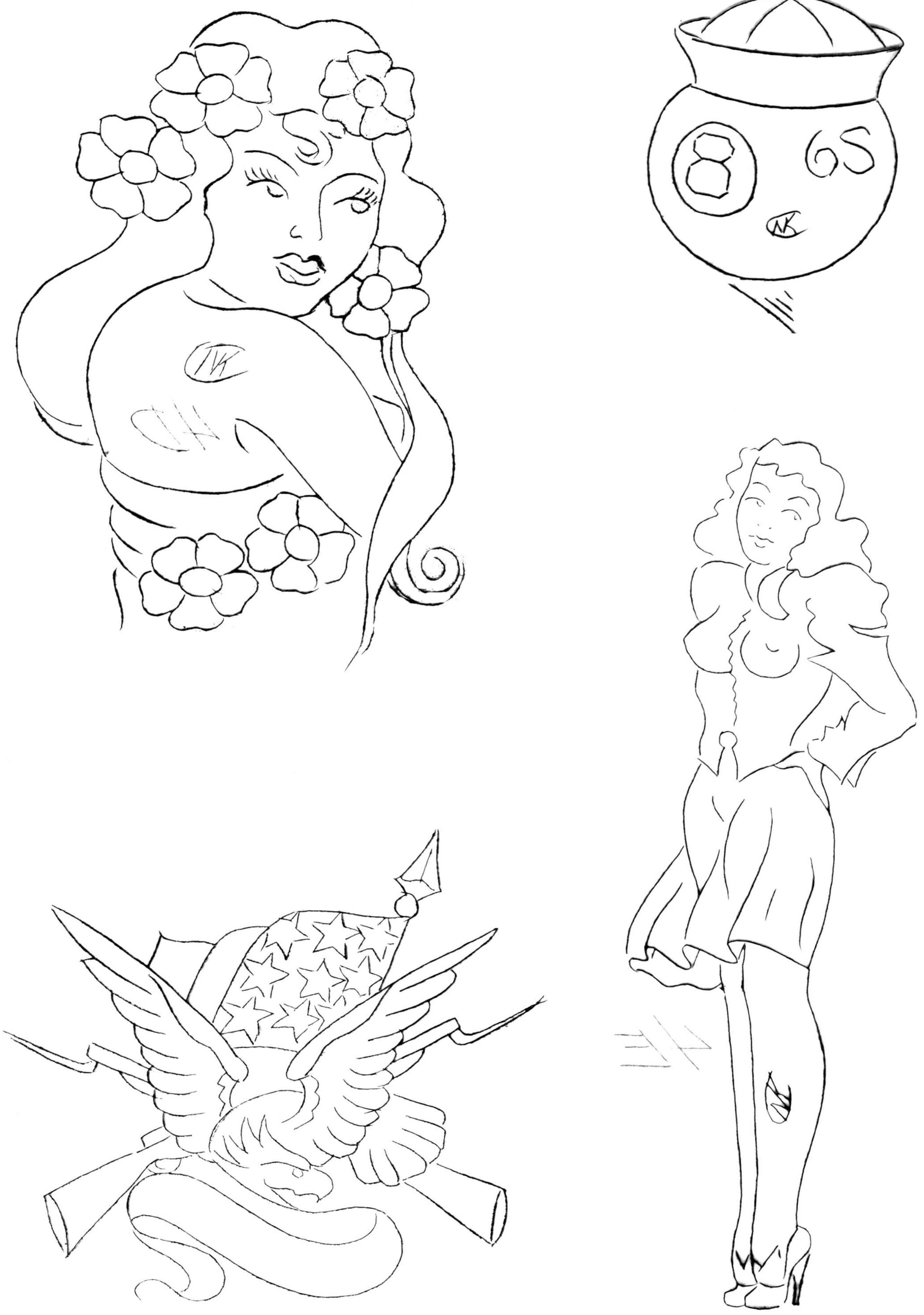

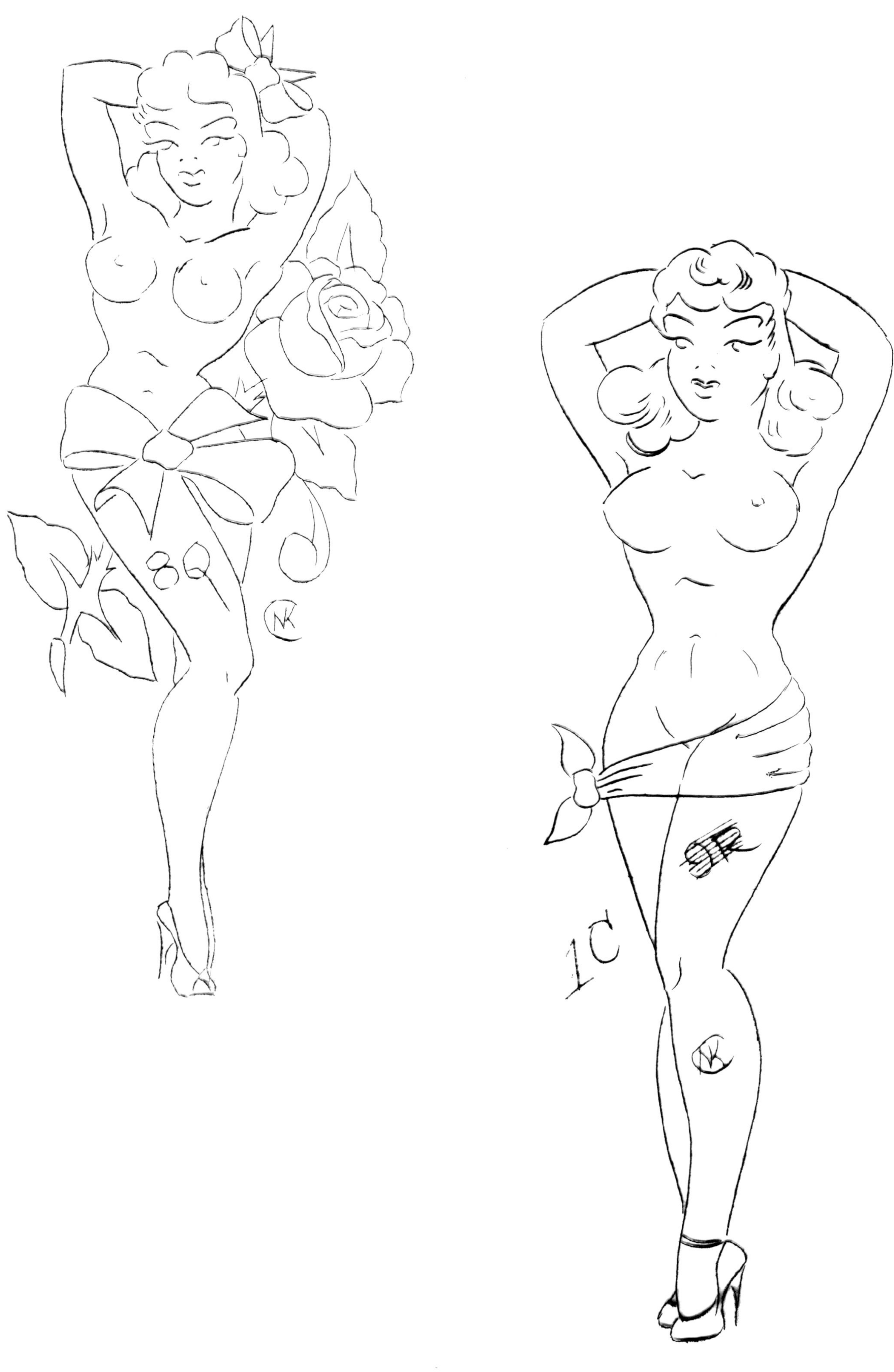
89
1C

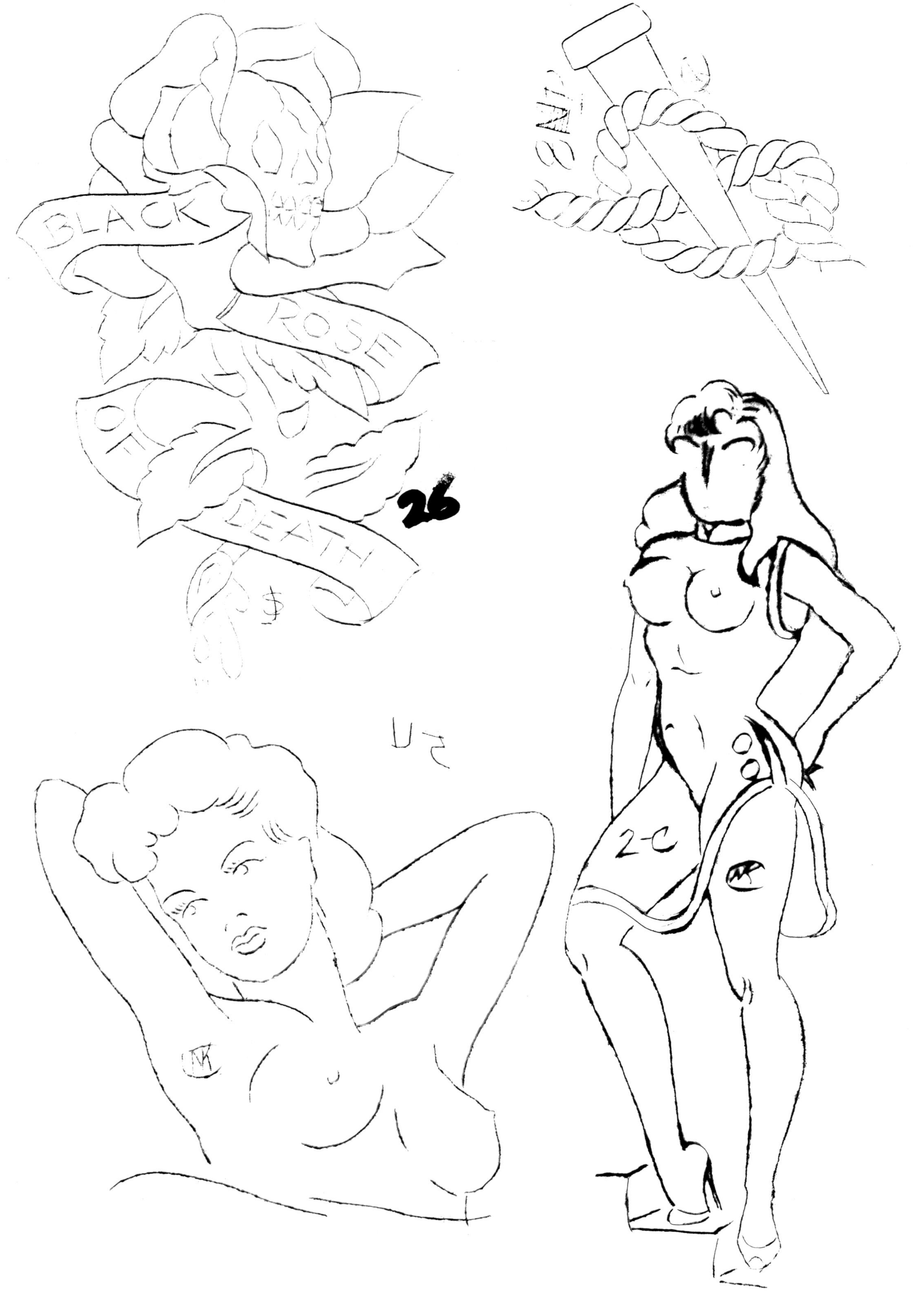
BLACK
ROSE
OF
DEATH
26
2-C

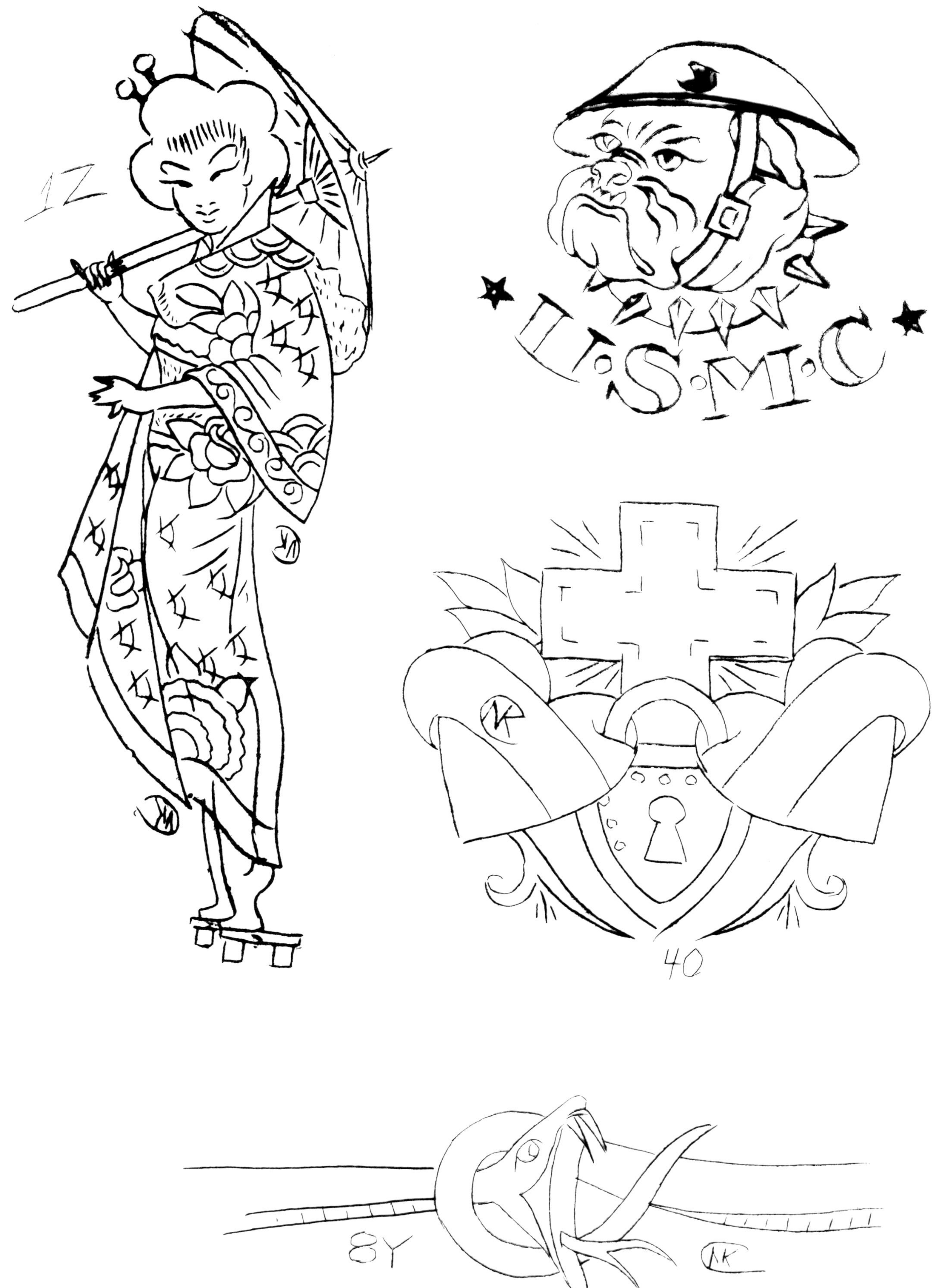

12
U·S·M·C
40
8Y

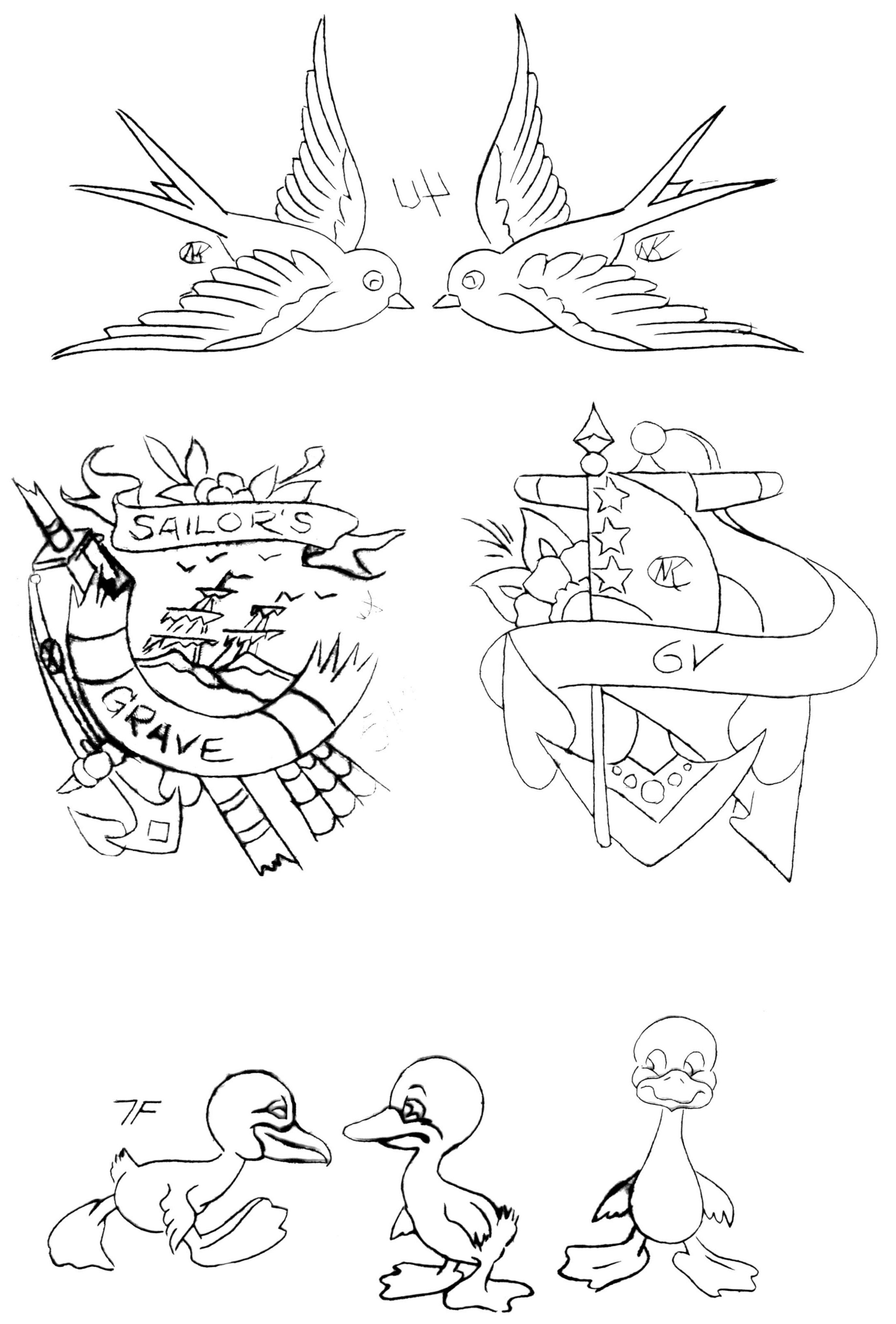

SAILOR'S
GRAVE
GV

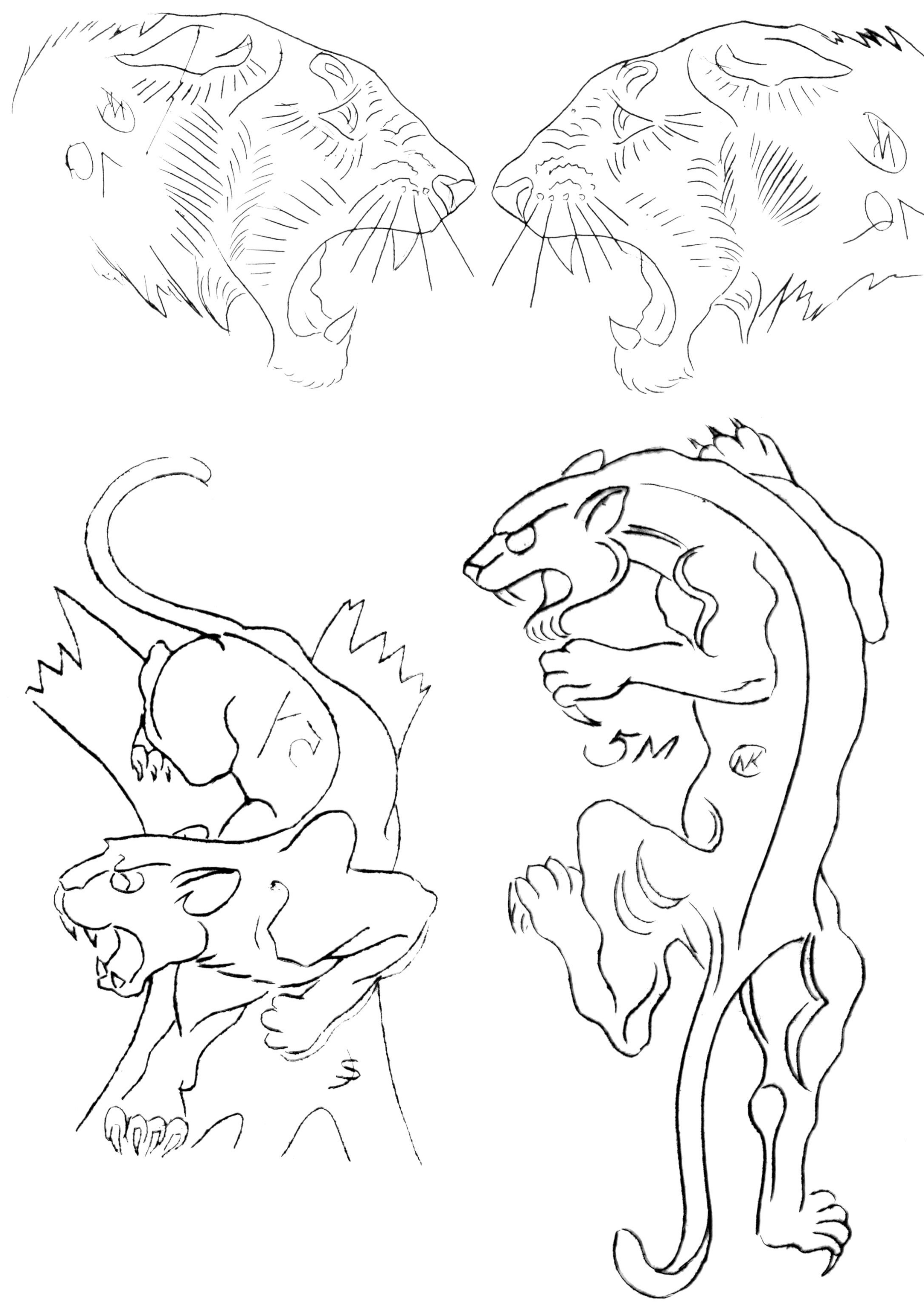

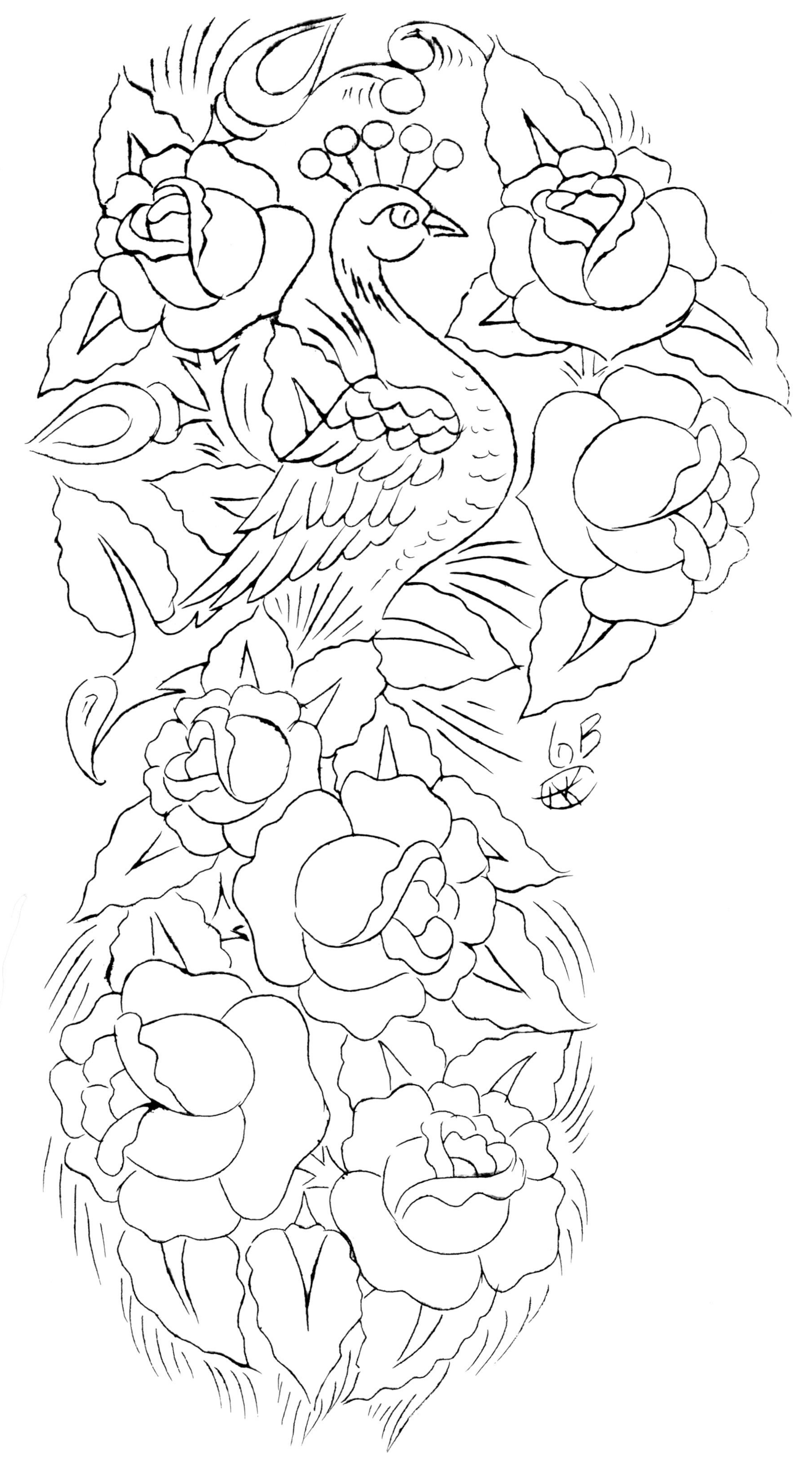

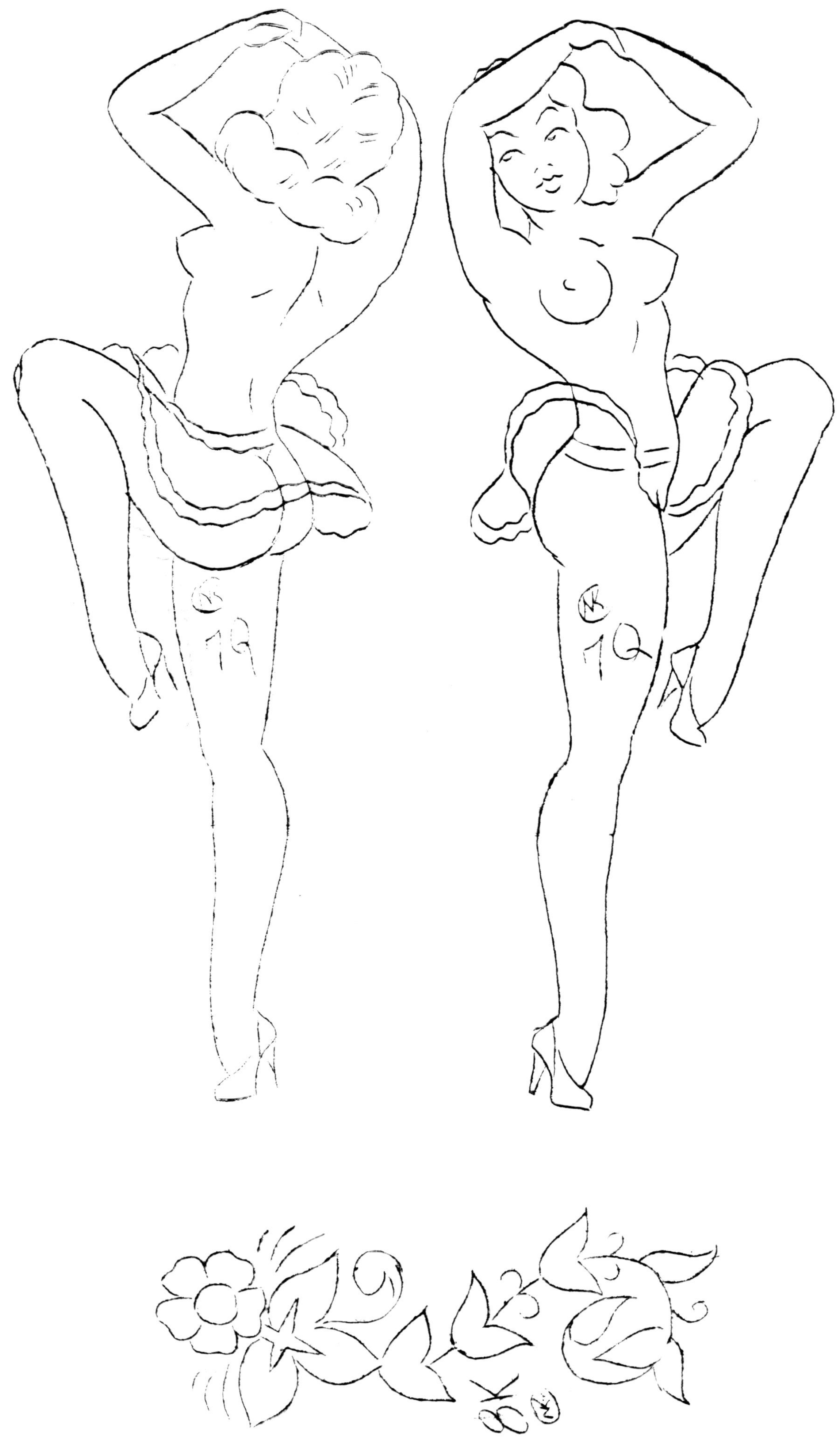

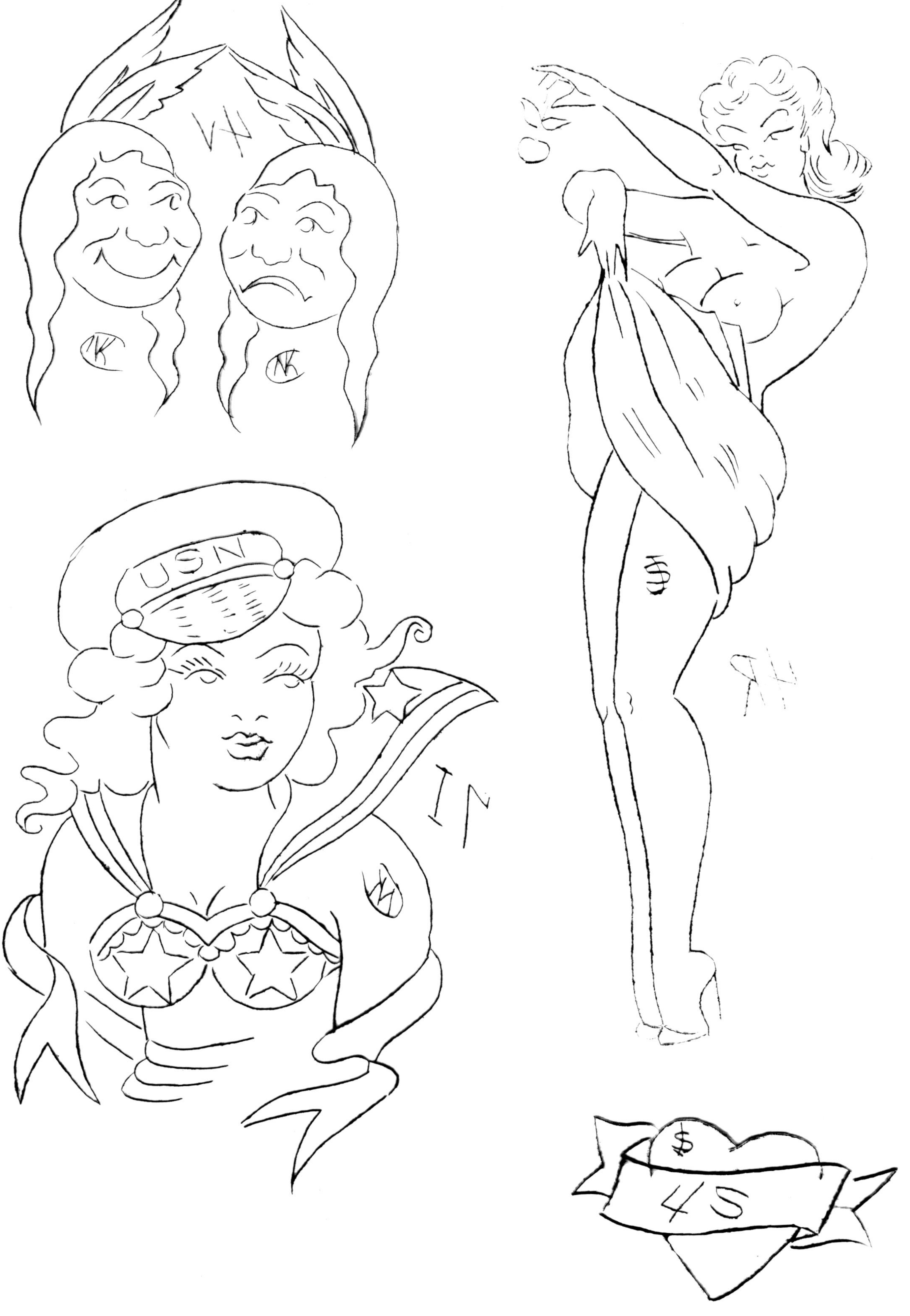
USN
$
45

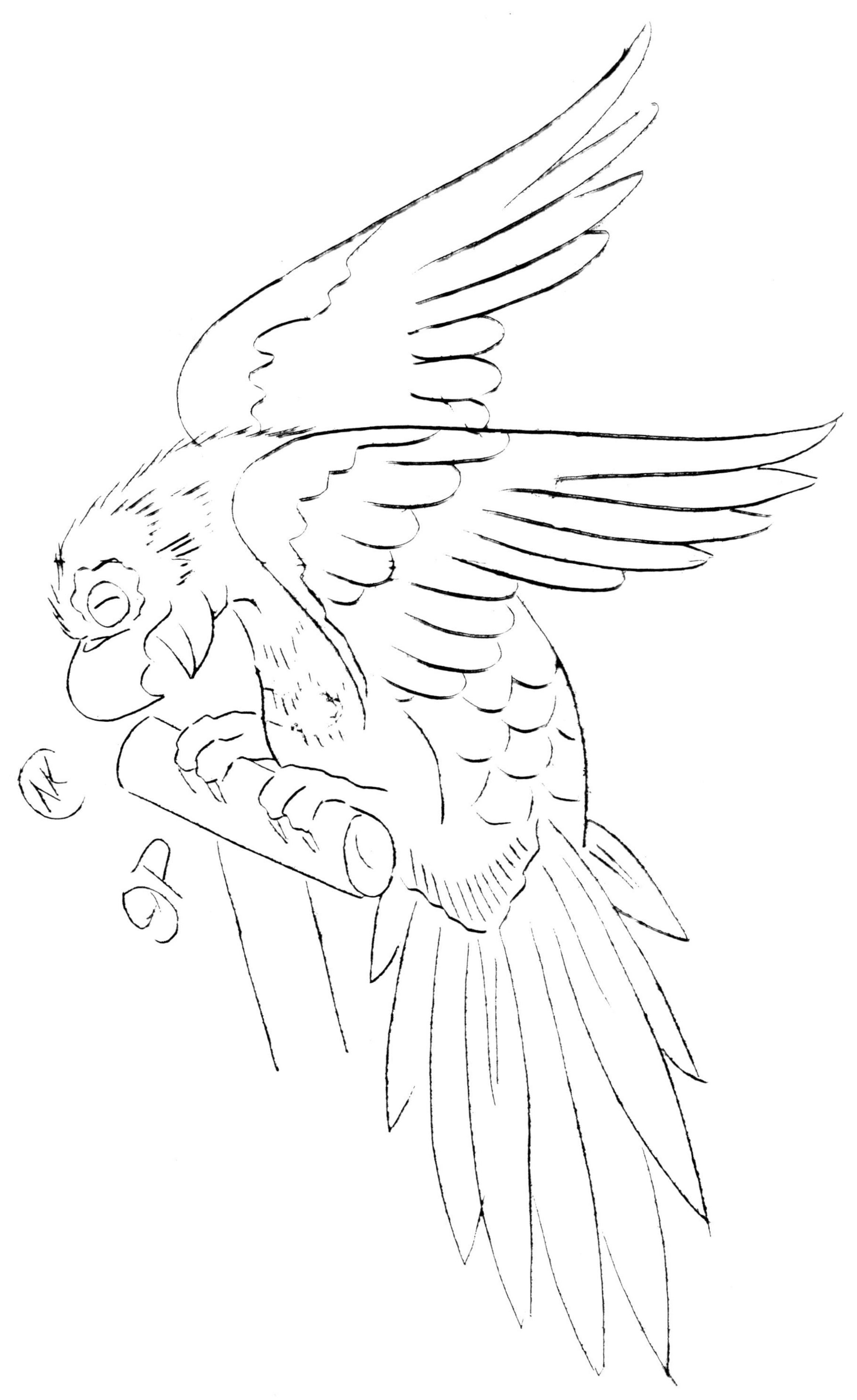

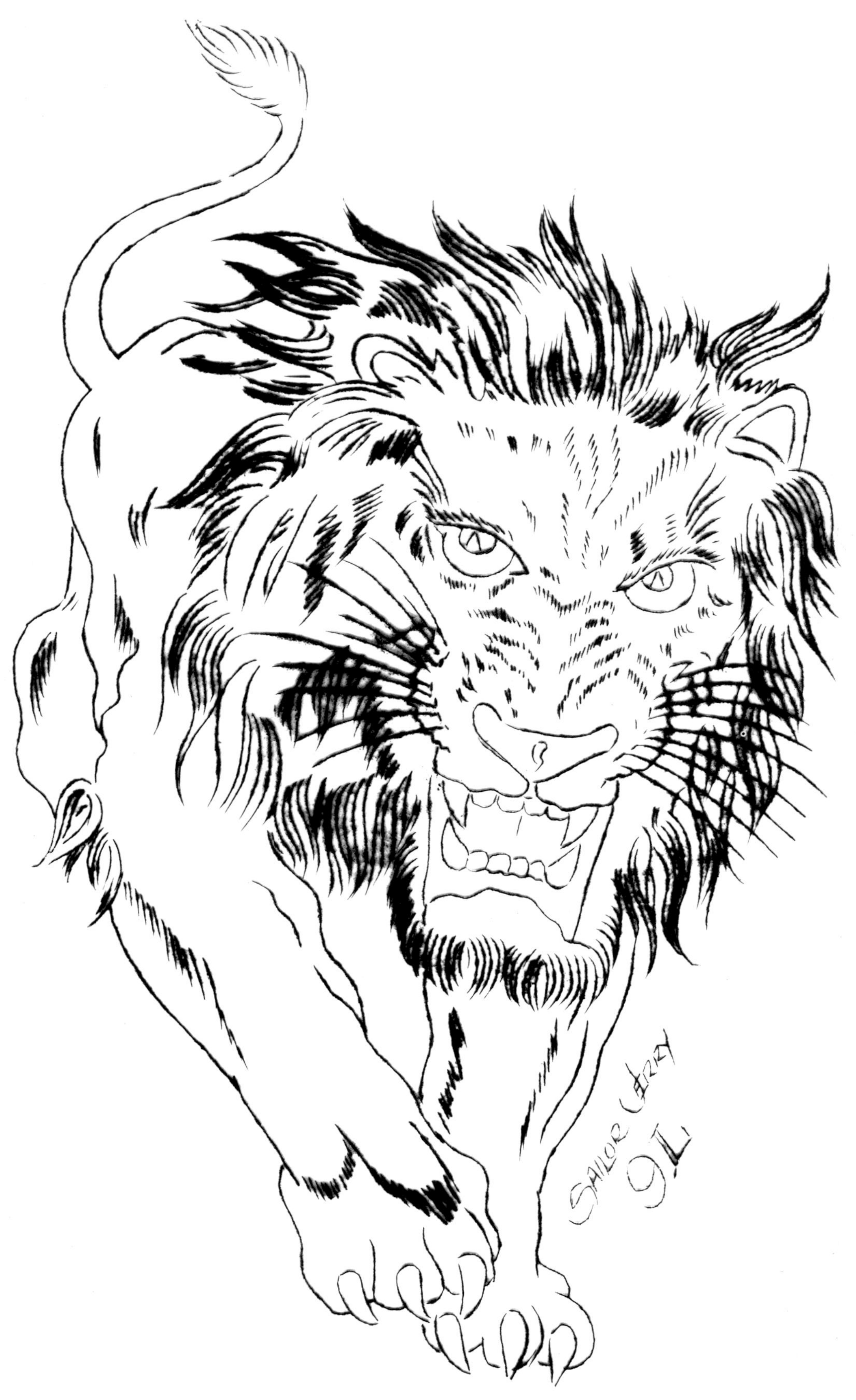
SAILOR JERRY